IN THE COMPANY

OF NEWFIES

RHODA LERMAN

In the Company
of Newfies

A SHARED LIFE

HENRY HOLT AND COMPANY

NEW YORK

Henry Holt and Company, Inc.
Publishers since 1866
115 West 18th Street
New York, New York 10011

Henry Holt® is a registered
trademark of Henry Holt and Company, Inc.

Library of Congress Cataloging-in-Publication Data
Lerman, Rhoda.
In the company of Newfies: a shared life / Rhoda Lerman. — 1st ed.
p.   cm.
1. Newfoundland dog—Anecdotes.   2. Dogs—Anecdotes.
3. Lerman, Rhoda.   I. Title.
SF429.N4L47   1996   96-6227
636.7'3—dc20   CIP
ISBN 0-8050-3746-2

Henry Holt books are available for special promotions and premiums.
For details contact: Director, Special Markets.

First edition—1996

DESIGNED BY KATE NICHOLS

Printed in the United States of America
All first editions are printed on acid-free paper. ∞

1   3   5   7   9   10   8   6   4   2

With the greatest of pleasure I dedicate this book to Hannah Hayman of Ebunyzar Kennels, Allen Coit Ransome and Randolph van Syoc of Toad Hall, and Margaret Willmott of Topmast Kennels—all of whom have stood behind me and often in front of me and always by my side as I learned about Newfoundlands.

IN THE COMPANY
OF NEWFIES

In the company of Newfoundlands, nothing is hidden. I slip the halter of what I've become. They slip the halter of what they've been, and we live together, passionately, changed. We share our lives, my Newfoundlands and I. This is a book about what is possible between humans and dogs, a book about communion, commitment, and intimacy. This is a book about the dogs who look steadfastly into my eyes and move their lips in vowel shapes, speaking to me as I speak to them, because they want to be like me, because their life's work is not to be dog, but to be human. They observe me more carefully than I them. They are alert to every stirring of my body, every change of breath. They don't dream of running in traffic, of eating puppies, of digging a tunnel in the backyard in a return to the feral, the wild, and the distant. They dream of being with me, like me, lying with me, curved into me, each vertebra pressed into me, their great heads over my feet so I can't leave without them. They work to be human, to be other than what they are, something other than dog. And I work to be other than what I am. We stretch our limits and change our lives.

My Newfoundlands live my life as passionately as I live their lives. I sit in their kennel at a picnic bench and write. They climb on my bed and rest. We share space, food, blue skies, icy waters, snowstorms. When I am without them I feel amputated; a part is missing. The empty place it is missing from feels the pain. My dogs act as if they feel that way also, amputated without me, for we are parts of one another now.

⬥

In the rosy, unrippled dawn of the first day, I sit at the edge of my makeshift bed overlooking the whelping box and watch six newborn pups nursing on Molly's nipples. Molly is a Landseer: a white dog with black markings. The namesake of the breed's variety is the artist Sir Edwin Landseer, who immortalized Queen Victoria's black-and-white Newfoundlands in portraits. She wears a black hood, a black saddle blanket over her entire back. She is very elegant and handsome, with deep dark eyes and a sculpted large head. Her neck is slightly short for perfection. She has always moved beautifully, muscularly, on strong, balanced bone. As a pup she was saucy and charming. As a bitch she is powerful, commanding, confident, apologetic when corrected. She runs her family with a strong personality. Tonight she is a mother. I feed her vanilla ice cream by the tablespoon and she licks the cold, sweet wetness to regain strength.

I've crocheted six differently colored wool necklaces to iden-
tify the Landseer puppies until we learn who has what markings. But already we can tell the male with the ring around the
tail, the female with Molly's saddle blanket back, the female
with the three spots, the male with the shape of Africa on his
back. In a few weeks we'll be able to make guesses about their
personalities; at seven weeks we'll give them personality tests
before they are sold so that they go to proper homes.

I will be up watching the puppies all this night and many,
many more. The pups are unutterably vulnerable, pink in the
red cast of the heat lamps secured above the whelping box. On
late-night TV, news of the California earthquake is breaking. I
see bodies, live and dead, pulled from wreckage. The heat lamps
give off an emergency glow, mirror the flashing red lights of
ambulances and rescue trucks in Los Angeles. I watch the temperature, adjust the heat. Molly, unable to complete natural
delivery, had a C-section; four puppies were born dead. Each one
is a tragedy, and if I were to dwell on the deaths, I could not go
on breeding. I continue to remind myself to dwell on the lives
of the six we have, for one is now dying, its head weak on the
nipple.

Molly weighs one hundred and twenty pounds; her pups
weigh a pound. They are molelike, velvet sleek, blind, their
faces folded, ears closed. They know temperature, touch, taste,
survival. Their lives are fragile. Molly and her pups will be
watched around the clock for the next three weeks. Whelping
tales are replete with disasters. Pups dehydrate, chill, fade for no
reason. Molly might roll over on them, step on them. The goat's
milk in the bottle might be too hot, too cold; the heat lamps
above the whelping box too hot, burn out. The pups might

suffocate under the corner of a blanket, drown on the goat's milk when I bottle-feed them. Sometimes their systems just don't turn on, can't connect. Or there is an accident at birth. I offer Molly water. I can't leave a bucket in the whelping box because puppies have been known to drown. There are too many horror stories. Visitors, the few I allow, will have to wash their hands and remove their shoes. No one may pick up the puppies. They sleep on polar fleece throws and fake sheepskin blankets. Outside, the snow rises to the windowsills of this, the warmest room in our house. The temperatures are below zero, the winds bitter. The temperature in the whelping room is kept at seventy-five, the whelping box itself at eighty-five, both of which are too hot for Molly. Her tongue hangs out. She pants.

The dying one climbs back on. "Don't give them names," the vet warned, "until you know who lives." Even so, I name him Billy to give him the bit of existence I can. A rabbi told me once that the only power of prediction left to humans is in naming their children. "Billy," I whisper to him as I hold him against my breast, his head in the crook of my elbow. "Billy." Billy was eviscerated at birth, sutured, revived, but he has a thin chance. He is very beautiful and sad, already. Billy tries to suckle. His head drops off the nipple of the baby bottle. He struggles to return to it. I fix the belly band covering his wound. He seems to have fattened, filled out. He is the size of my hand. I feed him drops of Pediolite, of goat's milk. I try Veta-Lac, a formula designed for orphan animals. He has no interest. His ears are soft and velvety, like the petals of anemones. He is deaf, blind, dying. I hope he doesn't know. The struggle for existence, the gorgeousness and terror of it, is before me. There are analogy and metaphor in the drama of the earth-quake news unfolding and crackling as it is on the all-night news programs. Somehow, in the face of the gargantuan blindness of that earth-cracking act, to wrest these small and precious lives from the fist of the universe becomes sacred.

Billy has stopped suckling the nipple of the baby bottle I've offered him. His body is long and elegant, well proportioned. His markings are perfect. He would be a wonderful and noble male. I draw little circles in his fur to relieve stress. It works on larger dogs. The household sleeps, the snow silences everything. I pray for him. I want no one to hear me pray for this unimportant life. There are so many other human lives at risk. Even so, tears well. It's foolish, useless, sentimental, but his is the life that has been put into my hands at this moment. Molly watched as I lifted Billy from the whelping box. She watched me feeding him, threatening, watching, judging. She no longer watches. Perhaps she already knows it's useless. "Our Father who art . . ." I had never before thought so keenly of the words. Our Father who art, our Father who makes, who crafts, who creates. The word *art* means more than "is." It means *makes*. I am part of this sacred act, this sacred breeding, this art. Like a priest, I watch over the sacred herd in the small hours, watch them struggle to life, to fullness, their bodies rounding as Molly's milk fills them, their breaths light, their tiny parts perfect and fragile as crystal. I am part of Molly's art, of a universal deed, a penultimate creative act that is sacred, that Molly shares with me. The name of our kennel is Blue Heaven. The name comes from the song: "Just Molly and me and baby makes three. / We're happy in our blue heaven."

When Molly came into season, Champion Topmast's Checkers, the sire of these puppies, was flown down from Saskatchewan. They met in Buffalo. Molly comes from a noble line of Newfoundlands, stringently bred, internationally honored. It is Checkers's line as well. Canadian and American Champion Topmast's Pied Piper—Molly's great-grandfather—and International, World, Danish, Italian, American, Austrian, Champion Topmast's Blackberry Blossom—her great-grandmother—are legends of the Newf world. Piper, who is listed on Molly's pedigree nine times, is spoken of in the worshipful tones normal people use for movie stars. Blackberry Blossom, was, I've heard, one of the most beautiful bitches in Newf history. I flew to their kennel on a ranch in Saskatchewan, on six hundred acres of brittle winter prairie, to choose Molly's husband for this litter. Over the dining room sideboard of John and Margaret Willmott's home, where an ancestor's portrait would be, Pied Piper's portrait hung. Margaret is as much a legend as her Topmast champions. Checkers is a sound and handsome Piper grandson who, it happens, was born on my birthday. Champion Walden Corbett Jorgensen—Molly's grandfather—was a grandson of Champion Topmast's Pied Piper. There is enormous potential for greatness in this litter, from many ancestors. But now, in their first few days, there is potential for loss.

The pups sleep at Molly's nipples. She shakes gently, stands very cautiously. I hold my breath. If I direct her out of the whelping box, over the wood slabs, I might steer her incorrectly. I have to trust that she knows precisely what she's doing, that she won't hurt her puppies. Fastidiously she cleans the whelping box, eats the excrement, licks the urine, then herself.

Molly steps out delicately, deliberately; she knows where each one is without looking, but she looks behind her once as if she can count—and perhaps she can. Then she climbs up beside me, licks my face for permission to sit on my bed, licks my face with the same tongue she licked afterbirth, shit, urine. (I am the pack leader. In the pack, she is the alpha bitch.) It isn't easy for me to let her lick my face, but it is her language and I must listen or she will stop speaking to me. Because I've learned to listen, my Newfies have continued to speak. That is the difference between my Newfies and the legions of other dogs I've owned. The Newfies have patiently insisted that I listen. I lie down. Molly lies down with me, curves every weary vertebra into my chest, belly, groin, presses as tightly against me, into me, as she can, sighs, shudders with exhaustion, and falls asleep. She snores. We will be awake again in an hour. We are mothers together. She smells of life. It is not clean.

In the whelping room at the veterinarian's office, when Molly first went into heavy labor, a young vet suggested I leave her alone, let her do her thing. There was no way to explain to him that we are intimate; that we have done everything together. That we have pierced each other's worlds. That I am— what?—her other half. She is not only dog and I am not only human. We are other than that. Newf owners struggle to explain this. A simple man who had come to breed his bitch with my stud said, "She took me through my divorce. She's a human in a fur coat." A breeder said, jokingly because he was embarrassed by his emotions: "We used to have dogs. Now we have Newfoundlands." There is some intrinsic difference that we all understand but cannot bring to words without sounding foolish. I think it is their commitment to us, their deep and abiding friendship. I sat with Molly at the vet's office. I dropped Rescue Remedy—a homeopathic stabilizer—on her tongue, offered her water, honey, yogurt. She leaned her head on my knee, looked in my eyes, and then, looking somewhere inside herself, pushed out her first puppy. It is the one that is dying now. Her placenta didn't come loose as it ought to have, and Billy was born eviscerated. The vet, holding him in his palms, blood leaking through his fingers, dashed past me to the operating room. If Billy had a chance, it was given to him. We do not take these lives lightly. "Billy," I say the word softly. "Billy. Next time, Billy."

The puppies whimper, sound like seagulls. It's time for Molly to return to the whelping box. I push her off the bed. She groans, climbs back on the bed, presses hard against me. "Go, Molly. You've got to." She climbs into the whelping box, lies on her belly, snores. "Roll over, Molly," I whisper. She rolls over. The puppies feed voraciously. I pick up Billy, hold him to the warmth of my chest, feed him goat's milk. We do our sacred work together in the strange light, the California earthquake flickering in the drift and sift of news and soft news repeated again and again as the night turns. I watch. Survivors are pulled from the wreckage as Molly's pups were pulled from the womb.

The rest of the pack, five of them, sleep or keep watch in the hallway just beyond the whelping room. Three—Celeste, Ishtar, and Pippa—are Molly's daughters. Celeste had a crippling disease when she was two weeks old, but she has, through the finest medicine and homeopathy available, survived. Her sister Ishtar will very likely be a champion. She is beautiful and gracious.

Ben is their father, Molly's husband, even though Molly has bred her second and third litter with other males. Ben is her emotional husband. We call them Mr. and Mrs. Dog. They are very good friends. Pippa is a huge and gorgeous female, already having won points toward her championship, just beginning her career. She is a year and a half and does not yet have her mother's or Ishtar's bitch elegance. Toby is an enormous and handsome stud dog from another line. Together they listen to the whimpers, the suckling sounds, Molly's snores, mine, I'm certain. They know each twitch and scent of my body, of one another's. They sniff at the air, at the smell of placenta, blood, afterbirth, dog milk, goat's milk, the frozen colostrum I brought home from the goat farm for emergencies. Certainly they smell Billy, his infection, his death. I don't know what they can smell, what they can know. When Molly was in labor with her second litter, I smelled the same smell I had when my mother was dying. I knew Molly had dead puppies. My dogs can know without experiencing things. I suppose one could call it instinct. I would call it brilliant efficiency. That's why I listen to them.

Molly's daughter Celeste approaches, licks my toes for permission to climb the bed. Celeste has always been sickly, and Molly has favored her with privileges that her other daughters—Ishtar and Pippa, lusty, strong bitches—have not been granted. But tonight even Celeste receives a red-eyed glare from Molly, some arrow of heat, of threat. Celeste slumps, drops her head, turns away, and lies down in the line of dogs in the hallway. Molly turns them away from the door. She has made no sounds, no moves. There are rules that are unthinkably dangerous to break. Bitches, unlike males, fight to the finish. Molly, I know, would kill to protect her puppies, but there is no need. Everyone understands. When Molly had her first litter, on the first night like this, she gave me that red-eyed, direct, defiant animal challenge, that glare: *Get out.* It was terrifying. She had been a silly, amusing thing, a puppy, a young female. I hadn't taken her very seriously. Suddenly she was all-powerful. She could kill me. She always could have killed me. She gave me that glare and I left the room. This is her third litter. We are friends now, perhaps sisters, certainly family. Molly and I know each other now. We trust each other. We've come a long way together. We know each other's limits, habits, quirks, needs, fears, furies. I know what Molly wants most of the time because she knows I listen, so she tells me. Nothing is hidden in the company of Newfoundlands. I can have no secrets. They want none. Molly snores. I climb over her, sit in the easy chair, and watch the news repeat itself over and over and wait for the puppies' first day.

Billy is worse in the morning. His head falls; minutes, hours slip away. I try everything: sugar and water, honey on his tongue, Pediolite. I am only making him worse. He struggles away from my offers. His temperature is dropping. A dog's temperature should be 101.5. His is 98, then 93. His little self is quitting. My hands shake as I rub him. He is dying. I've never touched death. I call the vet. His phone, we find later, has been knocked off the hook and the answering service can't reach him. We leave message after message until at last I call another vet who is willing to help but says, even on the phone, the chances are small. I fill a cardboard box with hot-water bottles and piles of his neon print polar fleece blankets and tuck Billy in as deep into the warmth as I can and race with our incubator to the car and to the vet. The snow is high, the driveway steep and narrow with ruts. The decision to go is, I know, the final step. But I give Billy whatever I can. If it's possible to pull out a miracle, we will.

Billy's body fits into the vet's hand. The vet is exceedingly gentle. He slips a tube down Billy's tiny throat. I notice how pink his new little tongue and mouth are. His mouth looks unfinished. His stomach is blue and swollen. He hadn't been filling out as I had hoped, but swelling painfully. The tube erupts with the yellow lava of impaction. All I have fed him comes back up again mustard yellow, bilious in the tube, alarming. But he seems more comfortable. He sleeps. He is so sleek and well marked. I wrap him in his fine brightly colored fleeces, a gift of the gods, to be returned, unused. He is too weak. The vet says, "There is little hope but let him rest. At least he's comfortable now." I can't let tears flow. "Perhaps tomorrow . . . ?" the vet calls from behind.

Perhaps he'll die tomorrow? Perhaps I should return tomorrow? "What?"

He shrugs. "Call me in the morning," he says. "I'll keep checking on him." I leave as quickly as I can.

I don't want to leave. I have to let go because I have to go home and hold on to the others. "You'll come back, baby," I allow myself to speak to the icy window. "I promise you. You'll come back to us next time." He is dead by morning. I would mourn but there is no time to grieve and I am too tired. There is an odd isostasy among the population of Newfoundlands. Bitches don't take. Bitches absorb litters. Dogs' semen goes sterile in the heat. Puppies die. No matter how many are born, there is always the same round number of twenty thousand. It is as if the Newfy bank will print only so many precious images. It is as if we are allowed just so many, no more.

∽

The first three days in a puppy's life are critical. Survival is tenuous. Unconscious of day or night, we mark time by nursing or sleeping. The hours are endless, intense, our heads heavy, our eyes red. We are all so tired, Molly far more than we are. The whelping box is kept at eighty-five, far too warm for a heavy-coated Newfy whose body burns with the digestion of food and production of milk. Her breasts are hot to the touch. The room is stifling. Under Molly's labored panting, I listen to a jungle buzz, a glottal drone, a fall and lift of sound. Nights on the Masai sounded like this. I remember listening and thinking in our little tourist cottage, in my netted bed thinking, This is where life must have begun, all our lives. This is what life sounded like, this Ur-sound, these nights.

Molly won't leave her puppies. She cleans mouths and behinds, stimulates bellies, rolls them over roughly, licks them hard, her tiny, incomprehensible things, bits of life. My husband and I stand above, whisper to each other, "How does she know? How does she know?" I watch the strange, slithering blind, deaf creatures, not attractive, infinitely fragile. They burrow about, look inward into other skies. What do they see? They cannot hear. Tonight they are sea creatures in seal skins, swimming across their universe of blanket. Muscles come alive, ripple, new bones move, nerves twitch. They will see at two weeks, hear at three.

The whelping box is a six-by-six-foot wooden construction, two feet high with a door cut into one side into which we can slip two loose boards. The boards will eventually serve, when needed, to keep Molly out and the puppies in. I pay special attention to the first adventurous puppy who climbs out of the whelping box and often keep that one for its intelligence, athletic ability, curiosity, and confidence. It will be weeks before they are able to climb, weeks before Molly will leave them. Eight-inch uprights support a narrow shelf that runs along the interior of the box. This shelf stops Molly from rolling on her puppies. The puppies gravitate to the spaces under the shelf. How do they know to do that? Only when they are cold do they move under the heat lamps, pile up to keep one another warm. Indoor-outdoor carpet covers the first layer of the whelping box floor; newspapers cover the second. The newspaper of choice is the *Wall Street Journal* because it's far more absorbent than any other. The *New York Times* runs second to the *Journal*. We cannot save enough. Friends bring their collections. My husband brings piles home from the dump. Blankets cover the newspapers, leaving only a border of paper exposed under the shelving, at the edges. The puppies are trained somehow to those bordering strips of newspaper along the alleys of the shelving. They scoot to the papers to pee and poop. They pull themselves across the blanket with a savage determination, flinging their forelegs on the ground and pulling their rear ends forward, like caterpillars, snails, snakes, amphibians. I hear the scratching of toenails on the newspaper in the alleys of the whelping box. They will also be scratching Molly's breasts as they knead to suckle. I rub Bag Balm on her nipples. Their toenails have to be clipped every few days to protect Molly's nipples. Why do I refuse to call the toenails claws? Why can I not think of these creatures as animals?

It's a time for mistakes. The litter's fragility is my terror, my sole responsibility. They suck my thoughts as they suck Molly's milk. Any lack of consciousness could snap their tiny lives instantly. Will a heat lamp fall? A blanket suffocate? What is a fading puppy? What does fading look like? It is a phrase like "crib death": a mystery, a terror. Puppies simply fade away and there is nothing one can do to help them. Will I step on a puppy hidden by a lump of blanket? Will Molly fall asleep and roll on one? When Molly goes outside to pee or poop and returns, snowy and cold, will she chill her puppies? At this early stage the puppies have no temperature control. A draft can kill them. Will the cat come in and steal one while I'm sleeping? Why is that one not feeding? Is that one with the ring around the tail using his rear legs? At all? I live in a state of anxiety. And even so, exhausted, I drift away as they feed, shake myself awake, pull myself up painfully from my rift of sleep, count puppies.

The female with the pink ribbon over there lies limply. I haven't seen her on the nipple since lunchtime. Is she sleeping? I pick her up. Her body drapes, drops, over my hand. Is this fading? I pull up my sweatshirt and rest her in a fold as I mix sugar and warm water and drop it into her mouth with a dropper. I send the vibrations of eating, of surviving, to the baby. I rub her. She moves slightly under my hands. Her skin is too loose. She is dehydrated. The others are solid, packed firmly into their skins like salamis, round. My tongue works for her, mimicking what I want her to do. Finally, that tiny rose petal of a tongue, weak, welcome, explores the taste and returns for more and she drinks an ounce of sugar water. Rose Blossom, Rosie. That's your name, litter person, Rose Blossom. Two or three hours later, I have not taken my eyes from her. Is she sleeping? Is she dead? I sob. My hands shake as I wake her and put her on Molly's nipple. Molly looks up at me, licks her puppy's head. It's a good sign. She suckles. I watch through the afternoon. She sucks harder and harder and is with us. I'll watch this little one for hours. A little sugar and water and a life is saved? They live on such fine thin threads. I find myself grinding my teeth. I clench and unclench my jaws again and again. My husband brings me chewing gum to ease my jaws.

Molly's milk is slow to come. The puppies must be supplemented, so we all stay up for another hour while they drink from the bottle. We weigh them three times a day to determine their need for food, their rate of growth. At four days, the puppies have nearly doubled their weight and are growing exponentially. I think of that old classroom film of a flower blooming in which the long time period of growth is compressed into a few minutes so schoolchildren can see the action. These puppies grow like a film flower. They are larger overnight.

The male with the one black leg crawls across the others, over their backs. He may be aggressive. Like fortune-tellers, we watch for signs. Did the one with the gold ribbon stumble? Is he dragging a leg? Is his tail up straight? Kinked? Is his gait off? Are his bones too fine? Is the female with the pink ribbon around her neck aggressive? Is that right rear leg on the puppy with the red ribbon more muscular than the left? Are the rear legs straight? I rehearse again and again the old wives' tales: If the pads of the feet are all one color, he won't have the spots we call ticking. If the eyes look blue in the sunlight, they will be dark. The nipples closest to the head give sweeter milk.

How can I shut my eyes or think a thought other than that of their survival? Their lives are in my hands. A woman in Italy drowned five of her eight puppies by feeding them too much formula. Most likely the hole in the nipple of the baby bottle was too large, allowing milk to overflow into the lungs. One pup was so big, so beautiful, a magnificent male, she put him in the freezer because she couldn't bear to part with him. This work of breeding is not for the faint of heart. I am the faint of heart. Breeders produce four, five, six litters a year. It's a tough game, tougher than anything I have ever done before and as thrilling as anything I know. Does magic have to rhyme with tragic? Error with terror? It is as if there is something intrinsically balanced in the miracle.

I hear scratching. I've fallen asleep sitting up. The night has gathered itself into morning and we've all lived. My husband is in the room. He's been worried also. What woke me was the soft new claws scratching the metal surface of the baby scale. Weight is the indicator of survival: who is fading, who must be supplemented with formula. Does Molly have enough milk?

"How about the pink one?" I murmur from my stupor. I haven't been as tired as this since I had my own infants.

"A half ounce."

"Gained?"

"Gained. How did you know about sugar water?"

"I don't know. I just knew." I have a double nature: I know I just know. It is too convoluted to consider, but I am grateful for the tiny flicker of life given this puppy because of it. Concerned all my grown life with who I am, I've forgotten not what I am, but what I also am. Now that I have been in the parallel universe of animals, of origins, a place in which one just knows, I remember what I also am, and because of that remembering, I touch my own double nature, which lies someplace between animal and human, unintegrated, often at odds, going in different directions. I am too aware to be an animal, too far from Eden.

I drag myself upstairs to my bed. It's my husband's turn to watch while I sleep. Rose Blossom, for now, is out of the woods. I drift off thinking of the irony of that phrase: She is out of the woods, out of the wild, moving in the direction of house and home and humans, moving, as I have, toward a double nature.

My once lovely house is a dogs' house now. City friends no longer come for elegant country weekends. Victorian society architect Stanford White would roll over in his grave if he knew what was going on below his vaulted ceilings, arched doorways, leaded glass, Doric columns. This was not his intention. I suspect the house smells. I no longer know. Hairs rise and float from furniture as we move past. Each week we wipe caked slime from the gorgeous woodwork, pawprints from the doors and floors, vacuum hair from carpets. Ammonia cleans the dried slime on the gorgeous stairwell. It isn't easy to keep up. Things break; none are missed. I have too many things as it is. Gray carpets are cleaned often but turn brown quickly with footprint, pawprint, bellyprint. Even though stones fill the kennel areas and the approach to the house, dogs absorb mud, puppies make mud, dig holes, spill water. Neighbors don't drop in any longer. A playwright comes for lunch, looks us over in our sweatpants and dirty jeans, our stained sneakers, tells us we look as if we're camping out in someone else's mansion. We do not fit the background. We've given precise meaning to the cliché "Gone to the dogs."

∝∞∿

After their early morning bottle feeding, I help my husband weigh the pups on the baby scale in the hallway. He takes one to the scale. I take a second from the whelping box. Up until now we have taken only one at a time to the scale in the hallway, which is out of Molly's sight. As soon as all the puppies are back in the box, and we are clearly finished with the task of weighing them, she picks one up, holds it by its belly, her huge and treacherous jaws encompassing all but head and tail and little matchstick legs. Horrified, we wrest the puppy from her mouth as she looks directly into my eyes. I see no hostility, no agitation, just determination. There is a message. She wasn't going to hurt it. She is finally telling me these are her puppies and she's had enough of our intervention. One at a time out of sight is bearable. Two out of sight at the same time—something we had not yet done until this moment—was unbearable. They are of great value to Molly. The puppies have swum, pulled themselves in their odd, primitive locomotion, half earthling, half fish, into the channels at the edges of the whelping box. There they sleep, twitching, startled by a new muscle, the coming to life of a nerve. What curious magnetism directed them to the sides of the box, away from the smell of their mother? Later, as I read, Molly stirs and leaves the litter box. I hear her walk, not to the door to relieve herself, but into the kitchen and along the hall to the basement. I follow her.

The basement, which harbors the immensely unpopular bathtub and the terrifying blow dryer, has never been a place of choice for the dogs, but I find Molly under the stairs, inspecting, exploring, scratching in the soft decaying cement floor. I imagine she is looking for Billy. In Molly's last litter, three puppies were stillborn. We had buried them far from the property. When I discovered her that time digging under the basement stairs, I assumed she was looking for them. Last year when Ishtar had a litter, she lost no puppies. Even so we found her digging in the mysterious space under the stairs. It is odd that both Ishtar and Molly chose that one spot in an enormous basement of hidden corners and dark niches. Neither had done it before nor would again, except after whelping, returning to the light of the kitchen, their heads draped in cobwebs. I don't understand.

There is such mystery in my dogs, so many dark areas of behavior, intention, instinct, so many areas that somehow promise to illuminate my own origins, my own instincts, my secret animal self. What is it that Molly and Ishtar seek? I return to the days and nights of my labor, of my childbirth, of my infants, of the moment I woke up to find an infant beside me, that first moment when I became something that I had never been, a crossing of my own Rubicon from my individuality, from my self-centeredness, a land to which I could never return: my emotional stretching out, as shocking and enduring and often as painful as the stretching out of my body from childbirth. There is nothing I can dig up from my births to help me understand Molly's and Ishtar's preoccupation with the basement. I call Molly up, brush off the cobwebs, and send her outside. "What is it, Molly? What are you doing in the basement?"

When the first and worst days are done and the pups are five days old, they sleep for longer periods: an hour or two. After they've nursed from Molly's nipples, we offer them baby bottles of infant formula. They suck rapidly and powerfully. I feel their vitality in my hand, up my arm. It is a good thing. Their rattails are thickening, fattening, quivering as they nurse, their bodies round and firm. When they sleep, their rear legs are splayed out flat and straight. That's supposed to be a sign of good hips. Everything is a sign of everything. Knowing so little, I watch for too much. They are all on the same schedule, moving like a school of fish, relieving themselves, sleeping, feeding at the same moment. They fall from the nipples, sleep for a few moments, pull themselves forward to Molly. They have strength in their front legs, little in their rear. Again on Molly's nipples, they climb over one another's backs. The male with the black leg pulls himself horizontally across Molly's side; he pushes three off as he moves. When Molly jumps from the whelping box, they whimper, worry, search frantically, finally rest.

I think of survival as a force, an energy, like electricity, wonder in the fog of my fatigue how one can trap it with a lightning rod. I wonder if the elixir of survival is the ingredient in the Rescue Remedy the vet gave the puppies as they were born, to Molly as she labored, to me as I waited, wonder why the words *elixir* and *electric* are so similar, wonder at everything. When I traveled to India I was told if I stayed a week, I could write a book about India, but if I stayed two weeks, I could not. It is like that with the dogs: they become greater mysteries the longer I know them. I have stood at the shoulder of Mount Everest, in awe of the earth's thrust to the skies. I stand as awed by the little scratched hole in the basement floor. It has as much power, as much mystery.

Toward morning, the wind blowing furiously up from the lake, from the north, winter flies buzzing slowly and desperately around the heat of the whelping box, the electricity shuts off. I hear a tree crack, a door slam, and we are in the dark. The puppies have no heat. By the time I have decided to heat the car and put them in it, the lights come on again and the furnace roars reassuringly in the basement. I heat water in plastic bottles, lay the bottles in a laundry basket, and cover them with blankets. If the heat goes off again, I'll pack the puppies in the laundry basket, drive to the vet's, and keep them in his whelping room. I am yet again in a state of terror. During the Cuban invasion in the sixties, when my children were small, I sat like this and wished for an atom bomb shelter, thought long and hard about what to do. Now my jaws clamp up, crack; my temples throb with the tightness of anxiety; but the lights stay on, the heat blows up from the basement. Suddenly I understand what Molly and Ishtar were doing digging in the basement. They too were preparing the safest place, the most distant, darkest, untraveled place they could imagine in case of an emergency. The dogs have crossed their Rubicon, extended themselves into the universe, become caretakers, and, just as I had, learned to worry about others. It fills my heart to know this: We are mothers, no longer girls. We are different creatures from those people who are not mothers. In this respect we are of the same nature.

Molly is sleeping next to the daybed, the door of the whelping box closed to her. She isn't happy that I've locked her out, but my head was heavy with sleep and I had to lie down. Dead asleep, I sense her. Somehow she tells me what she needs. Did a sound startle me? I see her framed at the door. She has to relieve herself. Molly returns with a roasted leathery pig ear she had cached in some secret place. Blindly, a puppy moves toward her smell. Molly makes an error, a lesser instinct—protecting her food—supersedes the greater instinct: she snaps at her puppy, protecting her pig's ear. I retrieve it, hide the pig's ear far from the room. And I scold her: "Roll over, Molly." She does, a bit ashamed, I think, for she first covers her eyes with her paw, then, remembering the pups, holds that paw high in the air, rests a back leg on the shelf of the whelping box, giving all the puppies as much access to her breasts as she might. The pups grab the nipples, their tiny feet pounding angrily at the flesh around it to draw milk, little oil wells pulling the wealth from mother earth. When I bottle-feed them, I feel them push at the bottle in my hand with an angry, primitive power. There are so many millions of years we have to accomplish in the next six weeks.

The red numbers of the clock bleed: three A.M. Almost time for my husband's turn. At nine A.M. another puppy breeder will baby-sit until noon so we can sleep. I walk with Molly on the back lawn, linger in the fresh night air. The moon is full, the cold, crisp sky filled with stars. She finishes and waits at the door to go back in to her puppies. I would like to stand under the stars and think about where life comes from, where it goes, about the puppies' will to survive, about Ben's oncoming death, but there is no time for abstracts. I open the back door and

Molly runs ahead of me to get to her puppies. They've tucked themselves into the corners of their whelping box and are fast asleep. Life, remarkable, fragile, incomprehensible, is in the whelping box.

⚭

And Death is in the hallway. Ben sighs like a sad winter wind, deep vanishing sighs. I know he'll die soon. Does he know? Do the other dogs know?

Champion Skipjack's Tiny, C.D., earned his Companion Dog title by passing obedience tests. He was a sound and reliable dog. Tiny never left his master's side, stayed where he was told to stay, did what he was asked to do. Once a week he visited a school for troubled children, and at that school an autistic boy attached to Tiny. Tiny, in a way that is beyond our human logic, attached to the boy. Tiny's family moved from California to the East Coast, bought an old farmhouse on a lonely country road, and worked to restore it. Tiny, as he did every evening, lay in the front door and watched his owners work. He was in a long down stay when he suddenly bolted, raced into the rainy night, down the hundred-yard driveway, and onto the country road. He was hit and immediately killed by a truck. Tiny had never done such a thing, had never left his owners, had never bolted from the house. And there was rarely any traffic on that road. As the owners sat, stunned, trying to gather themselves, the phone rang. The boy's mother called from California to tell them that the boy had run onto the road and had been killed by a truck. It was, according to Tiny's owners, exactly the same moment Tiny had been killed, the same moment Tiny had run inexplicably into the night. As distant as Tiny was from the boy in the physical dimension, as close as he was in another dimension of Newfoundland attachment, he had known something beyond our abilities, something, I think and his owners and breeders think, that moved him to save the boy at that moment. Three thousand miles away Tiny had known. He had run out to stop the truck to save the boy. Tiny was attached to the boy in deeper ways than we can imagine. It is the way Ben, I am certain, is attached to me.

And I to him. I listen to every breath he takes. I hear him groan as he shifts. Is it pain? No, it's much too early. I promise him he will not lose his flesh, his muscle, his balance, his joy, his dignity. I kneel at his side, touch his head lightly, kiss his forehead. He looks up at me with his big human eyes. "If I can help you, Ben, beautiful Ben, you will not feel pain. I will watch you, watch every move you make, because I know you will hide your pain from me. But I'll know because I know these things too and I will protect you from it. Somehow I will give you the gift of sleep, final sleep, and somehow you will have to give me the courage to do it." I don't know how I will go on without that nose pressing against me in my sleep, without that density on the skirt of the fireplace, that presence that says I'm here for you, forever. "Ben, I'll keep a little male. Stay with us long enough to teach him what you are, what you know."

Ben lifts a paw and lays it on my arm, groans, and rolls away to sleep. I am so anxious for the destinies of the whelping box to proceed, so terrified of Ben's destiny proceeding. I want to stop time and hurry it up. I want the puppies to hurry with their lives; I want Ben to stay as he is, forever.

Molly's hormones didn't kick in immediately, so she was willing, in the first days, to leave the whelping box and rest with me on the daybed. But now that she has regained her strength from her C-section and her breasts are heavy and pendulous with milk, and whatever else had to happen in her body and mind has happened, Molly will not leave her puppies alone, not for a beat of a second. Nor has she been left alone with the puppies, for a second is all it takes for her to roll over and suffocate one. I don't leave until someone spells me, not for the moment of heating a cup of tea or formula, of relieving myself. It seems obsessive; it is obsessive; but I could not live with myself if there were such an accident. When Molly leaves the whelping box we can rush around and do a few things, but up until now we have had to drag Molly from the whelping box. Now, the puppies having reached five days, she is willing to lie beside it for brief periods, which means I can slide the boards into the door of the whelping box, which will keep Molly out, and sleep in the daybed. It's a broken sleep, but it is sleep and welcome. The puppies complain of their hunger in the night. Molly, snoring noisily, doesn't stir. I push her to wake. She groans, rises, rolls from the bed, and stands at the front door to relieve herself before she goes in with the puppies. I remember it all. I remember the deep sleep, the dream that I'd already fed my own infant, the exhaustion, my head dropping as I held my baby on my lap, nodded off. Dear, dear Molly, I know how you feel.

The dogs in the hallway lift their heads, stand back away from her to let her pass. Molly goes into the snowy dark. She's tired. But she comes in snow mantled, wet footed, comes in sprinting, dashes past the dogs to get to her puppies. I wipe her impatient feet with a dry towel as she shakes the snow from her head and back, looks over the wall of the box at her puppies. She noses them until they stir, squeal, and come wildly alert: Mom! She steps around them, looking for a clearing, finds it. One puppy is on the wrong side of her, between the wall of the whelping box and her back. He pulls himself up over her great nose, pulls himself on his belly to a nipple. The puppy weighs three or four pounds. Molly weighs thirty times that. She is a whale. Still he climbs, insouciant, over her nose, grabs a nipple, latches on, and starts kneading. She is his. I like him. I shall watch him. His leg looks like a black silk stocking.

They are so much stronger now. They rush to her nipples. Their tails are fat, straight out in pleasure as they feed. I see the one with the gleaming black leg climb horizontally over the heads of the feeding pups, knock each one from a nipple as he goes by. They fall off, squall and cry. He finds a nipple and feeds sideways, blocking the others. Will he be aggressive? Dominant? Is he the wrong one to keep? Is this a sign? I pull him down and position him vertically, put the others back on. Now all are lined up, tails out, pumping away. They work very hard for milk. I see what will be great shoulders pushing at Molly's side. Now and then one straightens up on back legs. They feed until they slip off and then belly to a corner under the whelping box shelf, onto the newspaper to relieve themselves. Where do they get such civilized habits? Molly will catch one or two between her paws, lick them, stimulate their bowels, clean faces and heads. They shudder, sleep up against walls, tight into corners, pressed up against one another. They are so fat now they can no longer fit through the upright boards that support the shelves. They scream when caught in a traffic jam on the avenue of newspapers. Then they fall sleep. Some never make it as far as the corners and the shelves. They lie twitching, peeping, on the blankets under the heat lamps, dreaming.

What can you be dreaming of, little things? The simplest explanation of dreams is that they are a replay of the day's events reorganized by a psyche that doesn't think in our logical daytime patterns. Anyone watching a dreaming dog hears the faint bark, sees the legs moving, twitching, hears the panting, assumes he's dreaming. He's chasing a rabbit. The newborn puppies seem to dream the dreams of the big dogs with the same muted sounds, half cries, whimpers, mews, legs moving, twitching, chasing rabbits and running in fields. But the puppies have never known earth. No rabbits yet. They only know nipple to corner to nipple, yet their legs are running. Are you dreaming the dreams of other dogs? Is there a species memory bank of experience in which all the Newfies before you deposited their earthly experiences, their knowledge, their character, everything they learned? Are you dreaming of that first time a Newfy saved a human? Are you learning there under the heat lamp about pulling us from raging seas? Is there somewhere an "Everything You've Ever Needed to Know to Be a Newfy" tape? When you open your tiny eyes, will you know me and say, "Oh, yes, they told me about creatures like you and what our responsibilities are. Oh, yes. Hi." Could it be, as you sleep, you're learning from some wonder tape how to be good dogs, how to run and hunt and fight and save and climb mountains and swim rivers? That you are learning dignity and responsibility, goodness, morality, mercy? Are you learning instincts? How did saving a human being ever become an instinct? One of you had to do it first, to learn it. You must have been with us a long time to care so much about us. My sleeping dogs and my growing puppies may be dreaming those old species dreams, dreams not merely of the chase, but dreams of saving me and my kind, of kindness and kin. I know they are not fearful dreams. The tiny barks are excitement, not alarm. There are no growls.

When Ben first came to me at ten weeks, I opened the back door for him while holding a cookie in my hand. I gave him the cookie as he walked in the door. For seven years he has examined my hand for that same cookie as he walks in the back door. I never offered him a cookie at the back door again, but he never stopped looking for it. During the eight-to-twelve-week period, anything you teach a puppy just once is remembered, imprinted forever. After the learning period in which everything is remembered, it then takes forever to teach the dog something new. Exaggerating, we say that after twelve weeks the puppy must be shown a new behavior three hundred times. Perhaps these moments in the whelping box, these weeks before they can hear, before their eyes open, when smell, temperature, and touch are all that is available to them, perhaps these long nights of blindness and silence are the times they are learning the old things, listening to the old tapes, learning things they will know forever.

⌒∞⌒

Because the day has turned dark early, a winter wind herding the heavy clouds in from the north to hang close to the ground, covering the lake and lower lawn in mist, and because my husband is watching the puppies, I bring the dogs in, towel them dry, feed them pita bread, which I toss like Frisbees through the air. The dogs smell woolly, that half homey, half stink of wet fur and dog oils other people notice faster than dog owners.

I am a one-man band, scratching, rubbing, nuzzling. Toby, restless, having proved one thing or another, catapults from the sofa, leaps fearlessly over the girls, and lies down next to Pippa. The two of them chew on each other's mouths, lips, cheeks, ears. If my skin were as loose and resilient as their skin, I would lie with them and chew. I think I would rather sit with my dogs at the end of our day in this peaceable kingdom than do anything else in the world. And we shall dwell together. A photographer visited once and sat in with us at dusk here in the kitchen. Molly climbed him, burrowed her head into his lap. We sat still without talking. Finally he said, "You could charge a thousand bucks for ten minutes of this. I have a friend who would give his life to sit here."

I turn on a tape recording my dogs have never heard: the sounds of wolves. Over the sofa in the kitchen there is an oil painting which my grandfather copied from the original. A black wolf stands on a snowy hill at night, looking down (long-ingly, I imagine) on a cluster of homes in the valley below, homes with soft, warm yellow lights and smoke rising from the chimneys. My dogs were wolves once—black wolves, now extinct. So I play the tape of wolves in the wilderness. The first sound is a single, lush, riveting howl of adult wolf. It pierces the room. My dogs rise from their sultry sleep, lift their ears. Ben swings his great head to the eerie sound, lifts his head up to the ceiling-sky of the kitchen, and howls almost involuntarily, a new tentative stirring of his throat as if the howl were happening to him. Then all the dogs, Celeste in the lead, the others tumbling over her, dash into the tundra of carpet and furniture, leaping, crashing about the house to find the wolf. They return to charge the kitchen, glance at the tape recorder, behind it, regroup. A lamp goes over. It has survived falls before. The dogs race through the hall toward the living room. Around and around. The tape changes to barking and yapping, a chorus of howling, of answers and questions. I hear the lone wolf cry again, then a chorus of puppies, then adult wolves. It is language, not noise. My kitchen pack, for they are one now, races down the hallway, certain there's a wild presence. Having raised no quarry, as if chastened by their pointless activity, they take their places on the sofas and at my feet, yawn, and listen to the songs of their ancestors, intelligent, free, wild. On the tape the wolf pups yap, bark in a harmony, a chorus of meaning. Adult wolves, deep, sonorous, sing back to the pups. Ben lifts his head, stretches out his throat, starts the warble that will open to a howl, pauses, looks at me.

"It's your song, Ben, sing. It's your song."

And he sings, watching me, as if he is, I imagine, betraying me with his wild presence, his other nature. I smile and touch the top of Ben's head. He howls a round-shaped, full-bodied howl that ends in a glorious elongated high note. He looks the way Molly had when she was whelping: listening to something inside himself, eyes slightly out of focus. Molly dashes into the kitchen. She sits for a moment and sings with us but her howl is weaker, hesitant. Toby is somehow off-key, less confident than

Ben, but his throat reverberates, pounds, and he belts out howl after howl. He stands on the love seat, searches the front yard, certain the wolves are at the door. The girls whimper, bark, answer, sweep again and again through the house. They are pure dog now, shedding civilized skins, domestic manners, back in the deep forests running wild. Humans haven't entered their lives yet. They are all in the forest primeval now, hearing the old information, back in timelessness, back in forever. What in my life could be like this? Speaking in tongues? The wind chimes tuned to ancient musical/mathematical scales, to Martian harmonies? What music would take me back to my Eden, to my ancestors? What time-shaped chants, what ancient wails, what hymns?

I sing too. I bark and howl, my head stretched back like theirs, the muscles and tendons in my throat quivering and quavering like the deep strings on my cello, and I am a natural, my throat reverberating, vibrating, and I howl and feel the taut muscles.

Ben stops howling, looks at me. I beckon him with my first finger. He comes over to me, watches me carefully, sniffs my breath. He had not heard me howl before. I give my next howl all I have, share with him the wild, joyous freedom of our Pleistocene sing-along. Ben sniffs my howl and then stretches his head to my face, to the corner of my mouth, licks my lips. It is a wolf pack gesture of respect, an acknowledgment of my rank and my belonging. We are a wolf family and I am the kitchen leader. Wolves sing, don't bark. My dogs are howling like wolves and I am not surprised. The American black wolf domesticated by the Indians as workmate and draft animal was known, up until recent times, as the Big Indian Dog. When horses came to this country, they replaced the Newfs as draft animals. There is another theory, not as neat, but more imaginable: Newfies are an ancient cross between bears and wolves. They were also called bear-dogs, and indeed, I would guess more Newfies are called "Bear" than any other name.

I touch Ben's head. "Big Indian Dog, that's your real name. Indian Dog, did they teach you their silence, their bravery, their compassion? Or did you teach them?" The Indian Dogs remained in Newfoundland and Greenland, and when European sailors discovered them in the far north, they became known as Newfoundlands. They are such an old breed, their characteristics so potent, that the disposition, the sagacity, the compassion, the heroism, held steady when they were cross-bred, producing the Labrador retriever, the Chesapeake retriever, the Golden— all kind, good, stalwart, loyal, and gentle water creatures. I imagine my dogs as Indian Dogs, imagine Ben and Pippa— Pippa, who seems so ancient herself—padding silently, bravely, wisely, powerfully, in the immensity of New World wilderness. I close my eyes when I walk with them now and then, see no houses, see no roads, imagine wilderness, feel the old freedom that must have been theirs. Even before Pippa experienced winter, she would not drink from a bucket without first sticking her foot in. She was breaking ice to drink water. She had never seen ice but she knew it. I watched her and I watched an ancient, learned action, a piece of history realized again and again.

Molly stops howling, cocks her head, hears her puppies, and leaves us. She pauses before the whelping room door to make certain no one follows her, looks over her shoulder at me to ask if I'm coming. I say, "No," by leading the other dogs to the back door. I watch them race into the snow, into their mysteries, into the woods, and I wonder if, awakened by the wolf calls, they need to shake loose the aura of our domesticity, of me, of the kitchen, and find a piece of the wilderness. Ben looks at me over his shoulder, turns, loops around me. "Come. You can come with us. Really." He winds the skein of his invitation about my legs, and although I'm squandering my precious time for sleep while my husband tends the puppies, I accept his invitation, leaving language behind, run with him into the woods.

It is amazing to me that I as a writer, gifted with language skills, have made my deepest, most intimate relationship without language.

∽∞∾

Molly is more confident, leaves the puppies for longer periods of time. I increase the amount of formula in the baby bottles. They sleep longer. Molly's daughters so want to come in the room, to hang their heads over the whelping box and watch the puppies. As powerful as Molly is, she is obedient to us, recognizes our authority, but otherwise is willful and unforgiving. Molly is a bitch. She raises her head and gives one of her family a look and they wilt backward. But one cold and dark morning Ishtar waits for me in the hallway, can wait no longer, dashes in. Molly stares her down, growls far back in her throat. Ishtar backs out, dashes in again. She must be with me. She lies down and curls into what she considers an unobtrusive ball and is at last with me. Molly leaves to go outside. Molly is willing to let her stay. We're all more calm now that the critical days have passed. Ishtar leaps onto the daybed and watches the puppies from her safe place. In fairness to Molly, I push Ishtar off the bed when I hear Molly returning. The safety of her pups is a life-and-death issue for Molly.

It is more than instinct Molly brings to the whelping box. I find Molly sitting outside the box, her head resting on its plywood side, just watching the puppies. Compelled by the perfection, the profundity, the devotion of her motherhood, I watch her in awe.

When we've laid down clean blankets in the whelping box, I lie with her and she licks me as if I'm one of her puppies. Molly mothers me, healing me like a sacred dog with her spittle while I draw circles in her fur, deep circles all over her body, and she twitches under my fingers, sensual, we are, and passionate. I escape into my animal self. Sex had been my only escape, perhaps play when I was a child. But now, a great mother grooming me in the heat of the new puppies, in a pool of creation, I am as safe as any infant, as trusting, as clean, as loved. I fall asleep under Molly's labored panting, then thrust myself back into consciousness. It is too dangerous for me to sleep here. Molly stretches, leaves me and the puppies, runs out of the room, stands at the front door, looks over her shoulder until I arrive to let her out. Knowing she'll be nursing the puppies for a while—they have cried for food, her breasts are filled with milk—she plans ahead. She runs outside to relieve herself, runs back in, and climbs into the whelping box to let them nurse.

"Roll over, Molly." Molly lifts her foreleg up to her ear, lays her back leg high on the overhang of the whelping box, stretches out to expose both rows of nipples. I wipe her bottom with a Baby Wipe, towel dry her belly where I can. When she is finished with her puppies, she'll leave them, blindly, perfectly, not stepping on any of them, and lie down next to Ben on the cool cherrywood planks beyond the whelping room. They are husband and wife, and they have been away from each other too long.

Life outside the box is so interrupted, so fragmented, so poorly planned. In the whelping box whatever happens, happens with one goal, one direction, in its own time. Each sign of development satisfies. Molly now allows visitors. Ishtar comes in and watches with me. Celeste comes in. Pippa comes in. At last Ben sticks his head in the room, hops on the bed, watches. I put my arm around him; he rests his head on my shoulder. I feel his eyelash against my cheek. "Look, Ben, do you remember when you were a puppy? Do you? Look. That one is actually sitting. Look, he's yawning. Look, he's rolled over. Look, he's sleeping on his back. Look, he's getting a little shaggy. He'll have a good coat, won't he? Look, look, look. Look, he's coming over because he smells his mother. Look, he's licking Molly's lips." I think back to the tube feedings, to the one who didn't start breathing fast enough, to Billy. I can't think back. There are so many things that can go wrong. What a miracle that they will stand and move forward, sideways, backward, mostly forward, on four little legs, the tail that will thicken and give them the balance they need. What a plan, what a magnificent plan. I want to see them run. When do they run? I watch Ben watching them and wonder what he knows. When I hold one to Ben's face, he races from the room.

There is a moment between a man and a woman, on one side of which they are strangers, judging each other, but for one reason or another—a string of words, a quick secret smile, a hot look, a phrase—the line is crossed and judgment fails. It was that way with Ben. He was one of nine black puppies sitting against bales of hay under a shed, lined up perfectly, watching my approach with the hungry curiosity only puppies have. A cat ran between us. Eight puppies forgot me and ran after the cat. Ben, who had one white paw and an angel-shaped patch of white on his chest, sat still and watched me. I had no idea he was the pick of the litter. I only knew that I would take him home.

Just beyond this front room where icy drafts cut the air and the leaded-glass windows rattle in the wind, Ben, now a venerable six years old, lies on a gray-and-pink Tibetan rug and stares at me. His eyes are steady and purposefully intent. He whimpers a pluck on the chord of his music. It is a high, tight pizzicato squeak-whimper that should come from a much smaller creature—a mouse, a mole. It is ridiculous so large a creature can make so small a sound. I say nothing, stay still, force him to avert his eyes. I don't want to open a discussion. He opens his mouth, pursing his enormous lips as I purse mine when I speak to him, and he shapes and reshapes that great toothy triangular mouth of his until it is a little circle: my size, my shape. He repeats, as best he can, what is already clear: he wants to be with me but is afraid to enter Molly's space because she will, we know, eat his face. Molly sleeps, snores. Ben makes his tiny sound again. Molly lifts her head and watches him.

I enter the argument. "Ben." He tilts his head to catch the flow of my words, every nuance of my meaning, emotions, intentions. "I can't leave Molly and the puppies. I know you want to go upstairs to sleep and won't sleep without me, but I must stay here and count puppies every time I open my eyes, every time she moves."

He gives me what I and a million other dog owners call "that look." He has asked me. I have to say no, but he finds a middle ground. He leaves the front hall, goes around to the living room, and pushes his nose against the closed sliding door between the living room and the whelping room, against which the bed sits. I slide open the door, pat the far side of the bed. Molly watches as he climbs on. They have known each other for years. Molly came to us when Ben was a year old. He taught her boundaries and manners. She slept between his front paws. Her grandfather, Champion Walden Corbett Jorgensen, who won Best of Breed at the prestigious Westminster Kennel Club Competition in 1986 and was one of the top winning dogs in the nation for three years, is Ben's father. Ben has the breathtaking nobility and the gorgeous powerful movement I saw in Corbett even when he was at the end of his years.

Ben spreads his legs in front of himself, neatly, close together, his rear legs tucked under him, his body taut, controlled. "Notice," he tells Molly, "I'm in a long down stay and I won't move. My legs are not here." Ben does not even glance at the puppies, although his nose is working hard to know them. He doesn't dare admit he sees them. When Molly settles back to her puppies, Ben rolls over and presses the curve of his backbone against mine, sighs a huge expulsion of air, snores, and then falls silent with a soft, steady rise of chest.

Molly allows him only a few moments, then lifts her head and stares at him. His eyes open and he rises, leaping from the bed. Perhaps he's too warm; perhaps he felt Molly's malevolent heat. He goes into the coat closet to sleep under my coats, among my smells. Perhaps he just had to know, even for that short moment, that he could be with me and that there is a reasonable space between yes and no, between mastery and communication. It is more than just politically correct silliness to call our dogs companion animals rather than pets. Ben and I had negotiated his settlement, and he goes to sleep. Given the choice, we both prefer communication, although it is far less efficient than mastery.

When the squeaks, the deep-throat growls, the warbling,

the ululation he's perfected from large round woo-woo-woos, the hand grabbing, and all other signals fail, Ben resorts to charades. Consider the mind-set of this creature who works for understanding. When Ben wants to go outside he brings a shoe to me. "They use shoes to go outside. I need to go outside. I must find a shoe." One night I was gone and a dog-sitter slept in the house. Too early in the morning Ben brought her a shoe. She told Ben it was too early and rolled over. Ben was not to be dismissed so easily. He didn't drop the discussion but ran around the house, up and down the stairs, front stairs, back stairs, finally reappearing with the next clue in the charades: a sock retrieved from the laundry room. "Sock is in the family of things they put on their feet to go outside." This is a sentient, intelligent, problem-solving creature who has moved his thinking into clusters, into abstracts. Gregory Bateson, with whom I had the brief but enormous fortune to study, told about a dolphin who would do trick A and get a fish. One day she did trick A and did not get a fish, so she ran through her repertoire of learned tricks. None worked. No fish. And then she leaped to the next level of intelligence. She made up a trick, a new trick. Invention is indeed the daughter of necessity, even for dolphins. She received a fish and then went mad with the exultation, twisting, turning, calling, excited by her own creativity. She had moved to "Do a new thing." Ben had moved to "What else means go outside?"

Ben is black, has a long, smooth, deep coat; a majestic head; dark, deep-set, soft, compassionate, utterly human eyes; velvety, active ears, which, when wet, crimp up as they were when he was an infant pup. He has a great domed head, a handsome profile.

He is an old-fashioned Newf. He is sound and solid. "He isn't a dog," my friends say about Ben. "He just isn't a dog. There's something in his eyes. He isn't a dog." A long-term breeder and trainer of therapy dogs told me if she were marooned on a desert island and had to choose one dog to be her companion, of all the dogs she'd ever known, it would be Ben.

Breeders admire him, call him "an honest dog, a good dog." He is all that. When he runs, he is an athlete: smooth, powerful, stunning. He is gallant, honorable, and moral. I've seen him enter dog fights not to join them, but to separate the fighting dogs. He stands between people who are arguing. He is, unlike his heritage, afraid of the water or hates getting water in his ears; I don't know which. He needs to be coaxed to swim although he will walk in the water. When I took him to a water-training weekend, he performed all the tricks: rescued me, pulled in the boat, and so on, but on Monday morning he had a terrible backache and wouldn't move. I suspected something. A few days later I took him in the water and swam with him. Diving under for a moment, I discovered Ben's secret: he was walking. He had been walking during most of the water training segments. Even though Ben has a fear of or a distaste for swimming, if I were to call out, "Help, Ben, help," he would leap in, swim around me, let me take his tail, and, after pulling me to shore, lick and clean my mouth, nostrils, and eyes. I ask him to save me only once a summer. I don't want him to think it's a performance trick. He has too much dignity to be my dancing bear.

I cannot describe him objectively. Through another's eyes I can report that he is beautiful. For a day each summer, a small traveling circus comes to town. The troupe pulls in at dark, sets up at dawn, runs two shows late afternoon and evening, breaks down, and leaves. Mothers bring children in their pajamas at dawn to watch the elephants set up the tents and bleachers. I brought Ben.

The circus was coming to life. Fog rose in puffs from the lake. The hoof stock, exotic and domestic, camels to goats, ate fodder, snorted their steam into the fog. A dozen small Appaloosas stretched and turned, whinnied, paced. Men hammered stakes. A long-legged, long-haired blonde stretched in front of a trailer. Ben and I walked through knee-high wet grass to the elephants and watched carefully as they worked. Ben didn't make a sound. I laid my hand on his neck. Ben knows what kind of animal he is and is curious about other animals. Ben grew up on segments of *Animal Kingdom*. The one tape he watched without taking his eyes from the screen for twenty minutes was a tape of the Newfoundland National Competition in Denver. At shows, he examines the big black shaggy Belgian sheepdogs. Are they Newfies? No, he sees their sharp, pointed ears. He will pull me over to Newfies he's spotted among the two or three thousand dogs wandering in the show ring area. Ben knows who he is, who his family is, what other animals are.

Ben drank in everything at the circus. I wondered if he felt toward these exotic creatures what I feel toward him—a universal companionship. We walked around the elephants' tent raising to an eighteen-wheeler. A small dog (whom later we found would wear baby clothes and ride on the back of a wheeling Appaloosa) carried on about Ben's presence, leaping and barking behind his trailer. Ben, solemn, attentive to me, ignored him. In front of us a keeper dropped each door along the side of the truck, exposing the circus's great cats in their cages. One by one the cats rose, stretched, and roared at the rising sun, glanced at Ben, ignored him with the same hauteur with which he had ignored the yapping dog. I felt Ben's shoulder pressed against my leg. There was no movement, no sound, from him. There is an expression in Buddhism called "beginner's mind." It means a fresh approach, a new approach, a clear mind without the baggage and bias of education and experience. As a hazy sun shimmered on the wet grasses and the great cats roared, so immediate, so exotically present in our suburban backyard, standing next to Ben, trying to feel what he felt, his awe, his openness, perhaps even his curiosity, his compassion, his animal-belongingness, I could reach a blinking moment of that beginner's mind.

When all the doors were dropped, the keeper walked over to us—and this is the moment that still brings tears to my eyes—touched Ben's velvet head, scratched behind his ears, and said, this keeper of the most beautiful creatures in the world, "What a beautiful animal. What is he?" That's how beautiful Ben is. I trembled with pleasure as we walked home through the wet grass, my eyes filled with tears. That's how beautiful Ben is, that's how beautiful Ben is to me. When I took Molly to the circus, she set up such a roar that the elephants stopped working. Molly, perhaps less intelligent, less trusting, more fearful, went home in shame. Molly is powerful but doesn't have Ben's nobility, his grace, his self-control.

Nana in *Peter Pan* wasn't modeled from a female Saint Bernard, but from a great male Newfoundland named Luath, who had a passion for babies and children. While the female Nana has remained in our childhood fantasies as the caretaker of our innocence, it was Luath who created the character. He was the beloved pet of the author.

Ben looks at me, moves his lips in circles, and tells me as much as he can. This must be the true, the good, the beautiful, this ancestor soul who lies outside the whelping room, where one of those puppies, and perhaps none, has the possibility to grow and be like Ben: precious seeds of greatness, blooming silver souls. Even though Ben isn't the sire, Molly carries much of his genes. Among the hand-size pups swimming on their bellies, flailing their legs behind themselves like flippers, moving in the strange ontology of sea creature in their sheepskin landscape, there may indeed be that nobility and presence. There may be another Ben. It is my duty to bring that next soul to fruition, a painful deed before me.

Ben returns from the coat closet, stands at the bottom of the stairs, lifts his head, stares into my eyes, and moves his lips, opening and closing them in my vowel circles at the small front of his great mouth. How he struggles to contain, control his dog self, to squeeze his great active beast self into my small, weak, intellectual, earth-ignorant sedentary self. He is trying now to tell me something. I listen to him, and often, most often, I hear him. Sometimes I regret teaching him to speak, letting him know I listen, bending to his persuasion, which can be exhausting. When he was a puppy, before I'd begun to listen, I sat on the dock while he splashed in the lake in front of our home. He returned to me, pushed my foot with his nose, and stood in front of me, waiting. "Take your foot and move it into the water with me. Come," he commanded as I had commanded him. "Come." Each time he speaks to me, each charade that works, thrills me, and, I would imagine, he is relieved to be understood. He knows me intimately. My physical actions are a language to him. When I lift a hairbrush to my head, he's off with the car keys dangling from his mouth. If I stir in my bed, he's at my side, ready for morning.

Obviously the cost of establishing the level of communication we have is a reduction of my mastery over Ben. It is a small enough price. There is a line between communication and domination, between play and mastery. It is very difficult for me to stay on my side of that line. Ben's first moment of communication was astonishing to me. I had taught him to sit, and for that I gave him a reward, a treat. I initiated the command; he obeyed. He was still a small puppy when I turned one day to see him sitting by my leg, chest out in his "I am very good" stance, head up. I was at the stove, cooking something wonderful. He said, "I am sitting. Please give me a taste of your food." He had initiated the command, turned it around. Did I continue to assume mastery? Or did I do as he asked? Hey, a dog asks you a question, you answer him. Of course I gave him a bite of my food. Food is an excellent subject for communication.

One of Gregory Bateson's stories is about a man who asked a computer if computers would ever think like human beings. The computer whirred and whizzed and printed: "Let me tell you a story." A joke is a story. Ben makes up a linear progression of events that haven't yet occurred, that he will make occur. They are his jokes. Buddhist that Ben is, he is at play with the universe. His favorite joke is butting me from behind. I will hear the pounding of footsteps, and suddenly he has shoved against my hip, leg, rear, and is off again at a new angle. His best "gotcha" joke came on a fall day, I standing at the sandy edge of the lake, Ben behind me, planning his moves. His approach muffled by the sandy beach, he struck before I heard him, shoved between my legs, lifted me up in the air as if I were to ride him, took me a few feet into the water, then ran through my legs, and splashed deep into the shallow turquoise icy lake. He'd hip checked me on both legs at once by running up the middle.

I think the joke that most satisfied him, some ultimate moment of play, was one he played upon me and my twin sister. On a snowy night, my twin sister and I walked down the lawn toward the lake. My sister, visiting from Florida, was dressed in my winter clothes. Boots, coat, hat, gloves, probably her skin and blood, smelled like me. Ben could well imagine I had become two. Indeed, in the house he had watched us talking as we sat on the sofa, watched our faces back and forth, back and forth, listening, studying. He knew there was something unusual about one of us, but which one? Then we dressed and walked out into the backyard, down through the path of the rose garden. Ben lingered behind us, and then, his feet muffled by the snow as they had been by the sand, he must have barreled down the lawn after us, for he came from behind, raced between us, and spread us both: a glorious double hip check. I had to think he'd planned it. People say dogs live in the present. Ben has a longer stretch of consciousness. He had planned the moment, waited for it, imagined it, plotted the exact configuration of the bump, knew his width, the distance between my hip and my sister's hip. And got us. He was playing with me. He had told me his dog joke.

Since most of Ben's jokes result in black-and-blue areas on my body, I was happy when Molly came to live with us and bore the brunt of Ben's jokes. When she'd had enough of his bullying, his wild surprise dashes and hip slams, she'd snarl and lunge, and he'd shrink backward, grow small, and try again. I, caught by surprise and delighted, could only pull myself off the ground and laugh as he licked my face to make certain he hadn't, God forbid, hurt me. If Molly and I are both on the lawn, Ben will go for me first. Recently I had to go to a skin doctor for a facial problem. When he'd finished examining me, he asked me to strip so he could examine the rest of my skin. There was a moment when he saw the skinscape of nicks, bruises, old purple stripes from claws when we swam together, a history of physical contact. I looked as if I had been beaten. "What is all this?" he asked, waving his hand over my body. I felt like one of those Hungarian fencers, proud of my scars.

∞

Ben's first scent of love came on a summer night from a lovely bitch named Maggie. Ben stood tall and straight next to her, sniffed her rear, danced around her, licked her ears, her lips, begged, whined, and Maggie danced with him. Ben announced that Maggie was definitely in season. Her owner, Ann, put Maggie in the van immediately so she herself could sip iced tea on the back porch. Having lost Maggie so suddenly, Ben sat at Ann's feet, whining, growling far back in his throat, ululating, talking, making every sound imaginable to convince her that it was his universal duty to mount Ann. Maggie was long forgotten. Ben didn't move as he had with Maggie. He spoke his words of love to Ann. Ann laughed, embarrassed at her own sex appeal. She giggled. Ben persisted, barked his need to her. Ann left.

The next summer I was training Ben at a neighbor's house, and Ann, whom he had not since seen, came from a driveway a good hundred feet from our training spot. Ben went on alert, broke lead, and dashed to her. It was the woman he had decided, that year ago when he was so young, he loved. Ann was his first love.

If indeed our Newfs think of themselves as us, as human, not dog, which is of course how we think of them, it isn't surprising that instincts welling up may be focused on others of their kind, their kind being, somehow, us. Hand-raised gorillas grow up unwilling to mate with gorillas but masturbating every time a woman walks by their enclosures, being especially attracted to women similar to their surrogate human mothers. "You meet all my other needs," these double-natured animals question us, "why not this one as well?" One hand-raised chimpanzee, acutely aware of the division between animal and human, was given a set of photographs of animals and humans. She gathered all the photos of animals in one pile, all the photos of humans in the other pile, and added her own picture to the pile of human photographs. Whether she thought she, although an animal, belonged with the humans, or she thought of herself as human, I don't know. But I suspect, as Ben does, the chimpanzee thought of herself as one of us, of our kind, as human.

When Ben wants to take me someplace or he wants me to take him someplace, he grabs my hand at the wrist and pulls.

It's a firm, toothy grip. Is this disobedience? A lack of mastery on my part? Ben leads me to the garage for a cookie, the refrigerator for a piece of American cheese, the back door for a walk, the front door for a ride, upstairs to my bed for a nap. Once—he was not yet a year old—we walked out onto the ice of the lake in the cove. At the most, the water under the ice was a few feet deep. He did not want me to be on the lake and furiously pulled the sleeve of my winter coat. I reprimanded him again and again. He persisted. I finally shook him off and stepped, as he knew I would, through the ice into the water. Another time he took my wrist and had me halfway up the lawn. He would not let me go into the woods to walk the path we walked every morning. When I finally put him into his kennel and returned to the woods, I found an enormous white pine had crashed to the ground sometime during the night. The fallen tree no longer constituted a danger, but Ben knew, somehow, that something was wrong, out of place, and therefore possibly dangerous in the woods. A dog's eyesight is very bad. I've often seen deer on a path and turned around before the dogs noticed them. If I hadn't seen the fallen tree, certainly Ben hadn't. He knew.

We took him to a state park outside Denver this year. We walked down a paved road. Ben never leaves my side. Often, answering the phone means running his obstacle course. And I find myself staying in one place when I don't wish to because Ben is sleeping peacefully and I know if I move, he'll feel he has to also, and I hate to disturb him. In a strange place Ben is particularly knotted to my being, so it was with surprise that I saw him duck under a fence and march rather slowly into deep grass. I thought perhaps he was going to relieve himself. His nose was to the ground. But he walked too slowly, too carefully. At one hillock, he shrank backward. He was stalking something. I couldn't see grass bend. I became uneasy and called him back. Although he could have come under the fence at any point, certainly at the point I was standing, he oddly, cautiously, returned to the point he'd entered the field. A ranger arrived in a truck and told us that dogs weren't allowed in the park—the fields were filled with rattlers. I know Ben had sensed danger and gone out to measure it and protect me. The ranger told us many dogs had been killed by rattlers. We left immediately. In the car, Ben moved forward and licked my face and hands with great energy, as if he'd rescued me from a stormy sea. I knew what he was doing. So did he.

What kind of creature is he that he envelops me with his earth genius to protect me? Watching the younger dogs idolize him, obey him, defer to him, learn from him, I begin to wonder if religion and ritual spring not from a heavenly being, but from the venerated father of a tribe, for his ways, for his presence, from his powers. Ben is such a god in his kingdom.

❧

Ben is good. A few days before Molly whelped, Ben had to have a biopsy. Sniffing my own alarm, he resisted going into the back room of the vet's. Nothing pleasant had ever happened to him there: ear staples, stitches, shots, cages, acupuncture. He planted his feet and pulled his head back. A Newfy has been tested to pull at least three thousand pounds. The lab tech looked at me. I said, "It's okay, Ben. Go on." And his body relaxed and he trotted after the lab tech. Frightened or not, he would obey me.

I think he also needed permission to leave me, to accept another person's authority. Soon I am going to have to give permission to Ben to sleep, to die, and he will need permission because he can't rest until he is certain I am resting. In the night I feel him touch my nose with his. I hear him sniff. "Yes, she's breathing. She's there. She's fine. If she's okay, I'm okay. I can rest." I don't know how soon. Six months, a year? The thought is unbearable. At the vet's in the whelping room, I was told the results of the biopsy of the lumpy lymph nodes on Ben's scapulae were positive. Ben had lymphosarcoma.

I knew exactly where Ben got it. I had had thyroid cancer—the sort one gets at my age because many babies of my generation, particularly on the East Coast between 1936 and 1938, were irradiated in the thymus, and I was one of them. The cancer was infarcted when it was removed. A month later I had to swallow a radioactive drink to scan for any remaining cancer cells. I kept Ben with me in the bedroom, left the girls in the kennel, and never left my room. Toby came in once, felt, knew, intuited something, leaped away from me in alarm, and would not approach me for a week. It is not that Toby is cowardly. Ben's instinct was surpassed by his responsibility: he had to stay with me. Toby is simply more of a dog and less of a person.

Within a month Ben's lymph nodes at the back of his legs and under his scapulae were swollen. There is no oncologist who would consider the possibility that the radiation would have created Ben's cancer. And yet it would be Ben's way to receive my poisons, to take on my illnesses, to cure me. As coincidental as it may seem and as scientifically improbable, it is also terrifyingly odd that another woman who raises Newfies, who also had thyroid cancer and the ensuing radioactive drink, found lympho-sarcoma in her male Newfy, Flint, within a month of her drink. Flint had shown signs of the illness, but it was not detected because a bitch was in season in the kennel and that smell kills male appetite. Flint's loss of appetite—and, hence, his illness—was masked. It would be too late for Flint. The same vet found Ben's nodes much earlier in a routine exam.

Many oncologists explained patiently that it was impossible for Ben to have contracted lymphoma so quickly, that for humans there is a long latency period of ten years or more between radiation and the development of cancer. And yet? Perhaps my own cellular growth rate, Ben's growth rate, and lymph cancer's growth rate combined in such a way as to overwhelm his cells very quickly. Oncologists say politely, "Anything's possible. We need more than two pieces of evidence." I don't. Did Ben and Flint take on the mutations of our radiation, absorb the death frequencies into their systems? Toby knew there was danger coming from me and ran away. It would not be like Ben to run from the rattlesnakes. He would have to stay with me.

There is so much life and death compressed in their short lives, in this house tonight. Billy's death hovers. It is a terrible loss of potential. But Billy and I aren't in love. Billy doesn't know what Ben knows. You see, Ben will grieve as he leaves me, and I won't know what to tell him, how to help him leave me. How will I reassure him? What shoe and sock can I bring to him to explain the final walk? He'll worry about me, about his family of dogs, about his work, about who will take care of us all, who will defend us, his people, his wife, his children, his property, about who will tell us if the ice is weak or the tree has fallen. I will have to tell him it's okay to go, his work is done. It will be my terrible job to give him permission. And I will grieve because he won't be with me to take care of me. We have learned to count on each other. He is father, mother, lover, brother to me, skin. And beyond that, he is my guide in the wilderness of ice and forest and storm I don't understand. But if Ben knows about the ice and the tree and the storm coming, perhaps Ben knows about his death, about the end of things, that whatever happens between us is okay. When he was six months old Ben contracted a painful disease. No medication worked. No test gave us positive results. We were blind, and the dog was dying. The vet came again and again to the house as Ben's fever raged, as his lungs filled. On the last night, the vet told me Ben might not get through the night. I sank down next to Ben on the kitchen floor and slept with him as he struggled for breath. He couldn't lift his head. When I gave in to noisy tears, he lifted his paw and touched my shoulder to acknowledge me, to comfort me, to show me respect, gratitude, trust. He went to Cornell the next day. His life was touch and go for three days. Then a young resident vet called to ask what Ben liked to eat. Chicken. Later that night he called back, jubilant with the news that Ben had finally eaten microwaved chicken breast. I brought the vet a chocolate cake. Refusing the gift, he introduced me to another young student vet, explaining, "He should get the cake. He slept in the cage with Ben every night." Vets could teach other doctors much about doctor-patient relationships. A dog like Ben brings out the best in people. I pray Ben will be with us long enough to teach a little male puppy how to be noble, how to exercise and restrain his great power, how to be good.

When I hear women saying their dogs are spoiled rotten—

and I hear it often—I delight for them because they hear their dogs and they answer them. One puppy buyer described herself as a "spoiler." In the human world, spoiler means someone who is ready for a fight, the accessory bar one adds to a sports car to increase its tough look. In the shady world of human-animal, it means someone who is ready to communicate, to listen, to love. Yes, they are less easy to control, more demanding of attention, disobedient, and all that, but they are communicating to this, my alien universe, their unknown. Toby's daughter Layla is the worst-behaved dog in our puppy class. Her owner, a social worker, is kind and soft, and Layla does not obey her commands. Layla, however, was just chosen Therapy Dog of the Year by the Delta Society for the work she does with children. The Delta Society studies animal-human communication. It is a vastly different area from obedience training.

My husband comes down the stairs to take over our puppy watch. I step into the hallway. Ben is up and out of the coat closet immediately. He takes my wrist and takes me up the stairs, to my bedroom, around my bed, to my side of the bed. As soon as I sit on the edge of the bed, deposited, he releases my wrist. "Sleep," he says. How can one deny that he has spoken to me? "We're both tired, and I want to sleep there on the hearth where I belong, and you must sleep where you belong. I can't rest until I know you're asleep, so please lie down and sleep."

I sit on the edge of the bed, fall onto the pillows, and pull the covers over myself. "Stay with me, Ben. Stay as long as you can. Stay long enough to teach one of those puppies to be like you." Ben touches my nose with his, sits on the cool brick of the hearth, stretches out his paws in front of him, and slides his foreparts down onto the hearth. He lands like a Boeing, the front paws up in the air. Soon he is sleeping without sound. I listen as my husband, who never lifted a hand with our own babies, lets the other dogs out to urinate, calls them into the garage, speaks each name as he or she gets a cookie. I hear the garage door close. The dogs are settled down for what's left of the night. The dogs have changed both of us. Now I hear baby bottles rattling in boiling water. My husband is going to feed the puppies.

In their second week of life, movement has increased. Like exhausted marathon dancers, the puppies stagger, wobble, tumble, roll slowly, their future lives of action performed at halftime as their dogdom unfolds and becomes. A paw lifts and pushes weakly at a belly. A little body leans against another. The other falls down. Their music is already written. Their bodies know the dance. They are simply answering it, slowly, sleepily. When at last they fall, they drop like ripe fruit, collapse to sleep. I hear a faint bark. Is it from behind the scrim of the theater of their lives, a subconscious dream bark? Where are you in your dream, puppy? What are you doing? I hold a female against my face. She licks my nose, opens her mouth around it. I am present. "Hi, Big Indian Dog. Welcome to my world."

On the fifteenth day I discover them walking silently, dreamlike, walking back and forth across the whelping box. It is as if I'm looking down on a sleepy town square. They move cautiously, with delicate steps, as if they are dreaming themselves, astonished at this new and upright world.

There is nothing more interesting in my life to do than watch the puppies. Visitors come. I ask them to bring their old *Wall Street Journal*s. I make tea, bring out the cookies. We watch. Hours pass. It is a magic show beyond words. The slow-motion fights have sped up. Not only are tails used by the owners, but now there are tail pulls and grabs and furious screams and barks. Seeing, hearing, they are separating out from one another. Three fight; two sleep. I worry for that moment when they'll be truly separated, when they will become single dogs, lonely dogs, when they have to make the break and become dogs in a family of humans. The puppies growl now, lean forward on one another, inspect each other for nipples. Here one finds another's penis, another's ear. I think they grow at night. They try to rise to their feet, push off with hops. It was indeed a real bark I heard, not a dream bark. The largest one, Rosie, Rose Blossom, pink collared, a fat, round, impossibly hairy pup with a triangular head, is telling off another puppy. She has barked a few times now. She is ferocious. They are ferocious. Their suck on my forefinger has the power of an undertow. With a terrible survival energy, they fight with me for the nursing bottle. At Molly's side, in order to get to the nipples of choice, they savage each other with spurts of power, knocking each other, sending one another rolling backward off the nipple, crying, shoving, pushing. There are almost enough nipples for the puppies, but as this well dries up, they grapple with gravity and fight for the next. The lower nipples are always fuller, but the pups prefer the upper ones. Maybe it's true the milk is sweeter up higher. At last all the little tails are curved and quivering, the sign that the puppies are getting milk from the nipples. Their tiny shoulders move up and down as their feet pump the flesh around the nipples to draw out milk. Molly rolls them over forcefully, cleans their heads and bottoms with her rough tongue. They complain bitterly. She holds them in place until she's finished with them.

I carry Rosie to the window. Her eyes are open, cloudy, but open. Three days later, while she lies on her back in my arms and I rub her fat little belly, Rosie squirms and wiggles and freezes. Her eyes flash with a coal black light. I hold her up to my face. I'm a smudge to her, I'm sure, a tiny indentation on her brain mass, but she tenses up, straightens up, drops her head, throws it forward to mine, and looks at me. She must see me, for she licks my nose, tentatively, then seriously, closing her entire mouth around it. I am interesting. I am possibly food. Food is friendly. She had seen me and tasted me and, for the moment, knows me. Does she recognize my prototype from her natal tape? "This is a human. Be nice." I weep as I hold her and nuzzle into her face. She turns her head away. I am too much. But I have been in a primal moment. I am new. I am discovered. I am a universe. "I'll show you the sky, little one. I'll sniff the storm with you. I'll show you grass and ripe berries. We'll see the world anew together, you and I. I will be young with you, again and again and again, no matter how old I grow, I will be young. With you. For a while."

She has leaped the boundaries of her primitive life, crossed five million years, and she is unafraid of this enormous naked white splash of face and huge milky blue eyes swimming before her. She is curious. She looks at me. Her body is silent. Is she thinking? What has she seen? All those million years between us are over and we know each other. By the next day all the eyes are open, some still cloudy, but some flashing and aware, all here.

"Puppy, puppy," I call from the doorway to the whelping room. Do they hear? It is the twentieth day of their lives. They lift their heads to locate me, try to gain footage on the slippery surface of newspaper in the alleys. They run to the little door of the whelping box where I stand. I am suddenly, joyously aware that they hear me, my voice, my presence, my footfall. I am. They have moved from blind intention to reaction. To me. Later in the afternoon, when I come into the room, they stop their play, freeze frame, then go on. I lift up Rose Blossom, press her against my shoulder, against my neck, feel her puppy breath, say her name to her. Rosie. I am. We are. I tune the radio to soothing Christian hymns. The next morning I walk into the room and say, "Puppy, puppy." Three lift their heads. I turn on the classical music station. They move toward the corner closest to the radio. Rosie stands still, lifts her huge head, and barks, barks at no one, at nothing, barks for the joy of barking, listens to herself, runs to another place in the whelping box, and barks again. I bark at her; do I imagine she looks at me quizzically? She barks back at me.

There is something essential about them now, substantial. They are in this world. Their tails wag. Now they use them as rudders for movement, as signs of satisfaction, as balance, but soon the tail wags will be signs of friendship. Soon these fragile things will be my friends, my protectors. Indeed, as my husband

and I speak to each other by the door of the whelping box, one comes over to the door, examines us, wags his tail.

We've stopped our compulsive weighing of the puppies. They weigh enough. They're fat and firm, full of energy. We've extended the whelping box by adding a small crate and a wire exercise pen. Now they race back to their old spaces in the whelping box to poop but sleep in the new open spaces of the exercise pen or curl up in the crate. They are den creatures, cave dwellers. They are immediately drawn to the safety of the crate. I drape it over with towels at night. Molly still patrols the whelping box, searches out and eats any excrement. I hope it's a hormonal action. I hope she doesn't really like it.

In order to air out the room, clean the carpets, and wash down the linoleum under the whelping box, we move the puppies and their housing, heat lamps, blankets, and newspapers to the garage for a day. The newspapers are spread in a different relationship to the blankets, by the door of the whelping box instead of at the back. The puppies run in circles, completely confused, and finally pee in their crate, which sits in the same configuration that the newspapers had in the whelping box. They had only one map, need to make a new one for this new space. Now they have two maps. Unless of course they dreamed some. The puppies are filling their brains with maps, sequences. I watch them adapt, stretch their tiny envelopes, explore, eat a dried leaf, the cardboard roll from the paper towels, a scrap of paper. A packing box becomes a secret den. They dash in and out of it, climb over it, learn "up" and "fall." We set the whelping box inside the house again, and the pups, relieved to be home, race into their corners, scramble down their alleys.

It is more and more difficult to convince Molly to go into the box and nurse the puppies. When I see her sitting up, then standing as the puppies nurse, I realize that they must have teeth and those teeth must be needle sharp. Poor Molly. Instead of every hour, instead of every two hours, the puppies are allowed to nurse on Molly three times a night. Molly stays with them long enough to clean them, clean the whelping box, and let them suck until they drag themselves into the corners to sleep. Life eases for us all. We suppose they sleep between midnight and six or seven in the morning. But I hear them at night, yapping, fighting, running around on the papers. At the most, we can be assured they are not crying out in hunger. At daylight we find them sleeping quietly, innocently, in their crate, but the blankets are mysteriously bunched together, the newspapers torn apart, the water bucket spilled. Like the dancing princesses of the fairy tale who secretly escaped the castle and danced all night, their worn shoes being the only evidence, the puppies have left evidence of a wild night. On my approach at daybreak, they race and tumble to the stretch of pen closest to the door, climb it, watch, whimper, beg, yelp, pile up, chew fingers, chew one another, fall off. Often in the melee one will sit back and stare into my eyes. I'll sense the stare and look down, and there will be those bright jet black eyes staring at me, learning, thinking, trusting, open.

Now when they fight, they fight full speed. They growl and bare their tiny teeth. It is only they who don't know they are puppies. They do everything real dogs do. We laugh at them because real dogs don't make mistakes, don't wobble and topple and fall down. So we laugh at their incompetency. Soon we won't laugh. Soon they will leap logs without measuring. Soon the earth will fall under their feet, make way for them.

Friend now that I am, I sit in the whelping box with Molly and the pups at night and feed a few from the bottle as the others nurse on Molly. They look in my eyes, lick my fingers, sit at my feet, and cuddle into my neck. Puppies burrow against my chest, find their way into the placket of my nightgown, and find the flesh of my breasts. For a brief moment I slide back into my beginnings and let them burrow against my breasts. For a brief moment I am their animal and nothing, no one, else. It is an ecstasy, a stepping out of my world into theirs. Australian myth sings of a time when men could become animals and animals could become men, and they understood each other's languages. There are times now, for me, with my dogs. Certainly the puppies think I am animal. I perhaps am more so than I ever was. My socks smell of urine. The room needs changing . . . everything. I pull out wastebaskets, towels. I want a bath, a long, solitary soak. I feel unclean. I take Molly to the basement tub and hose her rear and tail. I don't want to touch her. I don't want to know about afterbirth. The water running off her rear parts is greenish. I can't wait for all this to be over. I yearn to sleep a whole night in my own bed, feel clean.

❧

Everything is new again when you have puppies. I want to show them snow. I want to show them the sky, rain, a storm, a tree, the other dogs, the world. I want to share their first moments with them, see the world as they do for the first time, renew myself as they awaken, show them the apple trees, show them the lake, take them into my bed and cuddle with them. When? How soon? I roll the boy with the one black leg over on his back, stroke his belly. He clutches at my first finger for safety. The clutch is like suction, a primordial survival monkey clutch. I am a limb in the jungle and this puppy is a tree climber, grasping my finger to keep from falling. I am astonished at the power in the grasp. His name will be Silk Stocking if I keep him, Silky. He struggles on his back. It is not a safe position. He folds his forelegs over my fingers, tightens his grasp. I understand that shapes in the womb go from single cell to more complex organisms, then to recognizable fish, and so on up the ladder of animal life. Could behavior also climb the ladder of animal life here in the whelping box, from swimming to climbing to walking? From bee buzz to birdcall to bark? My puppies are swimming fish, then climbing monkeys. Soon they'll be competent four-legged walkers who bark. Perhaps they'll try to move their lips and warble vowels as Ben does when he speaks to me. Perhaps, perhaps, they will stretch and move up another rung, living with me, if I give them enough, if they are capable of taking more. Are they? Everything in me wants to believe they are.

In the lake, my dogs balance themselves on their rear legs, stand upright, tread water with their forelegs. Stand upright, reader, and look at each other face-to-face as if they were dancing or at a cocktail party. It is always astonishing to see them hanging out on two feet in the water. Ishtar was the first, the others followed her. Or perhaps I was the first and they stand because I do. The water supports them. I watch them, dreaming myself, imagining it was in water that apes became humans, just as my dogs, straightening their rear legs, walking, might be imagining themselves as being able to do what I can do.

One pup falls asleep on Molly's leg, one on mine. One is tucked against my thigh. I lift her and place her between Molly's front legs, the safest place. I've heard that the pup who sleeps between the mother's legs is her favorite. This one, Rose Blossom, is my favorite, my keeper. She is a hairball, a little Chia puppy. I have never seen a coat like this. She has a huge triangular head and a cloud of hair all over. She is either a freak or a beauty. She could hang from my fingers, her monkey clutch is so powerful. She is an exaggeration of puppy. None of the visiting breeders have ever seen a head like this, so out of proportion. "Who will you keep?" they ask. I look past the female to Silky, who is perfectly marked except for that one gleaming black leg. He has plenty of bone, a massive head already, a handsome and serious look about him. A white blaze runs down the center of his black head. "We'll keep that male," I say. "The one with the single black front leg, the silk stocking." Silky. Silky. In Molly's pedigree there is another famous male, Champion Hornblower's Long John Silver. He also had that one black leg. Maybe the black leg is a genetic marker for all the rest of Long John Silver's magnificence. Maybe it's a sign. We find his picture in a book. Yes. Keep the one with the black leg. Judges may not like it. It's distracting when he runs forward. Judges can't really see his movement. No, I'm determined. Silky. Still, the visitors want to take another look at the female with the triangular head and the exploding coat. "Let us know," the visitors say as they leave, "if you're keeping that funny female." I know I need a good male. I also know, in other ways, I am going to keep Rosie. I think there is something there in the female. I think I will have to keep Silky. The phone is ringing with customers. All of them want a good Landseer bitch. I want the money to pay for Ben's chemotherapy. I want both puppies. I want. I want. I want the male and the female. I want them all. How can I trust anyone to care for them as ferociously as I will?

∞

The pups are almost a month old. Just as I have, Molly has been confined with them all this time. Up until now, as soon as she's relieved herself outside, she's pawed, banged, rammed the back door to come in. But this morning she has stayed out and gone to play with the other dogs. I watch her from a window as she leaps into the snow, throws herself on her back, rolls in the snow, lies on her belly, cools the hot itch of her tortured breasts. Her family approaches her cautiously. She has been bristling with hostility all these weeks, but now she touches noses, invites them into her circle, allows them to smell her rear end, to know what happened. She is a depository of information. She is playful, frisky, runs after Ben. He sniffs her, knows everything. She tires quickly and stands at the door to come inside, runs to check her puppies. Satisfied—has she counted them?—she follows me into the kitchen and settles at my feet. I feed her at any opportunity, tempting her with pots of chicken and rice, pocket bread with peanut butter and wheat germ, oatmeal and milk. We worry about her nutrition, the pups. Now I find meatballs in the freezer and defrost them. For once she is ravenous. Encouraged, I boil a pot of pasta, shake in shredded cheese and milk. We hear the puppies yapping, playing. Molly devours the pasta in great gulps, empties her bowl, and trots off to the whelping room so purposefully, I follow.

Molly stands next to the whelping box, and carefully, precisely, regurgitates the pasta, and only the pasta, in a neat, steamy pile at the door of the whelping box. There is no retching, no shoulder activity, no sound of vomiting, no meatball. Hers is a polite and perfect delivery, a different sort of act from that of an upset stomach. The pile of pasta is her sign that she is finished whelping and her pups are to eat whole food. Grains now? Meatballs later? She no longer wants them on her nipples. It's time. Who has set this formidable clock in motion? In the wild she would have caught a tiny creature for them, a rabbit, a mole, and offered it to the pups, somewhat digested, warmed, perhaps cleansed by her stomach enzymes. Limited, she waited for the correct food to be offered her. Meatballs wouldn't do; chicken and rice wouldn't do; pita and peanut butter wouldn't do. The pasta would do. But where are the meatballs? She has somehow chosen to retain the meatballs. How?

The pasta is my sign also, and I assure her, as I clean up the pasta, that her pups will be on whole food in a day or two and she can stop nursing when she wishes. I have never found vomit magical until this moment: steaming, it is the incredible perfection of the universe, of creation, of a vast plan for life. The steaming mound of grain, milk, and fat is as focused, as imperative, as profound a religious experience as I have ever known. No amount of ceremony, ritual, study, no double rainbows or bleeding statues, no meditating, deep breathing, no prayer has ever given me a more specific sign of the goodness and the greatness of life. One turns inward or upward for a spiritual experience. My Newfs exist in a parallel universe, alongside, neither upward nor downward. Now and then doors open between us, and I experience the wonder and security of a universe that cares for its creatures.

During the fourth week, we fill custard cups with a mixture of Gerber's baby rice, boiled spring water, and goat's milk and, holding Silky's head, bring the cup up to him as we stick a finger in it. He licks the nipple-ish finger, then plunges his entire head to the bottom of the bowl and comes up covered. "Where is that nipple?" he asks, plunging again and again. He bites. He eats. I remove my finger. He's eating. Look at that! He is covered with sticky formula and rice. It is as momentous an event as moving from fish to amphibian. Nothing will ever be the same again. The pups sleep for three long and welcome hours after the system shock of real food. They wake with new energy, catapult around their area, climb each other, up onto the shelves. Molly steps into the whelping box, lies down, invites them to suckle. They do with savage furor. I cringe as I watch. When all are firmly attached, she rolls over and slings the entire family up in the air, like kids on a roller coaster. Hang on, everybody. I think Molly is playing a joke on them. Molly rolls back, flips them again. Still they hang on. Molly leaves the whelping box without cleaning it. She won't touch the poop from manmade food. Pippa sneaks into the room, slouching, sits behind the easy chair, and peeks into the whelping box. The puppies stand on their hind legs, lean over the top, and look at Pippa, sniffing, yelping. They assume she's Molly. Pippa glances quickly over her shoulder to see if Molly is watching, then stands, climbs in, sniffs each puppy. They try to nurse, and she is off and running.

The next step after individual custard cups is a large low plastic dish for everyone at the same time. The puppies sit in their food, slide across it with their exploding pleasure at the discovery of food without so much work. They still seek the nipples when Molly steps into the whelping box. She stands, restless, hurting, while the puppies hang on the nipples, stand on their rear feet, fall often, fight. Molly looks like the bitch who founded Rome and its seven hills. That bitch wasn't happy either.

They are so voracious, I divide the food into three of the plastic dishes. By nightfall they lap up the gruel as if they'd been doing it all their little lives. They've forgotten Molly's nipples altogether. Their tails are up, curved downward, quivering, satisfied, excited. When every suspicion of food and saliva is gone, Rosie steps into a plastic dish, chews softly on its edge, curls up, and goes to sleep. I lay more of the dishes in the whelping box. Three puppies curl up in them. I imagine them as flying saucers delivering puppies from heaven. I laugh wryly at my sentiment. I am all sentiment these days, all feelings, weeping, joyous, a strange high, a focus.

Just as I am turning off the house lights and locking up, I hear a noise from the pups. Silky has pushed his way out of the box, past the exercise pen, and is racing up and down the whelping room with a bright green washcloth in his mouth. He must have heard me, for he stops, steps onto the threshold of the room, and looks up to the high vault of hall ceiling, to outside, to another place, into my universe. I watch him staring upward, looking up and down the hall. I shall never forget him: tiny, brave, curious, backlit by the heat lamps, that green washcloth hanging from his mouth, he stunned by the vastness of what is beyond him. He is so small in the arched door, so precious, so ready. He runs back to the far side of the whelping box. I open a space and put him in with his treasure: his golden bough from the other side, his bright green washcloth, and I focus on the moment because I never want to forget it.

I lie on my belly, squeeze my eyes half shut, peer through the window of time, and watch them, imagine them, grown. The roseate lights of the heat lamps become the TV cameras at Westminster. I watch them at Madison Square, in the Garden, see them proud and noble in the ring, powerful, breathtaking, their huge fronts and shoulders rolling as they come forward, their backs straight, their heads held high. I am so proud of them already. This is my garden of dogs, blooming here on the snowy sheepskins, my flowers. The tail set is already there, the size of the feet relative to the length of leg is there, the height relative to the length is there. The long pelvis is in place to hold the great muscles, the neck is strong and thick, the heads round, the muzzles wide. Other people think I'm crazy. But there are a few of us who make our living as artists, not as engineers, not with logic, and we claim we can see it. I don't know what problems they will have, that are already drawn into their genes—bad knees, elbows, hearts? I'll care for them as I cared for my children, with full and fierce consciousness. Five million years separate us, but they come bounding to me through the silence. They are not us, not at all, but they will grow up in my garden and become my flowers.

At eleven P.M. we overfeed them. I've added more cereal to the liquid. Stuffed, they sleep the sleep of the just fed, spread out, on their backs, drugged, and I close the door to the whelping room. Ben takes my hand in his mouth, leads me upstairs to my bed, our bed. Molly follows, climbs in next to me. Ben lies down at the hearth, and we finally, all of us, have a full night's sleep.

The puppies want to chew, anything. They gleefully rip off corners of their newspaper bedding, hold the paper high, and race around the box, shoving and tantalizing one another. I buy them real toys: a small rubber squeeze frog, a shoe, a hedgehog, a Snoopy dog, a hot dog. Molly decides these toys are for her and immediately confiscates them. Or is that what she has decided? I know the toys disappear immediately. I am not accustomed to the dogs taking a toy except to play with it. I haven't seen them hiding toys. Most often they flash the toy into another dog's face to initiate a game of chase; if no one takes up the chase, the toy is abandoned. Toys have not been possessions in our dog family. I don't know what Molly's intentions are. Nor do I know where the toys are, but I don't search. This, after all, is her business as well. She walks past me, her mouth full, and I know she is carrying a toy, keeping it hidden, to the side, covered, twisting her mouth so it has a wry camel look at the lips. Finally I take advantage of my rank: I lift a flew and peek inside. She is carrying the toy frog. I drop the flew closed. Molly has a secret.

Our dogs often present a toy to us, push it into our lap or leg or hand, and ask to play. Not these toys. Something far more serious than play is on Molly's mind. Celeste sniffs at Molly's mouth, receives a low warning growl, and backs away. The other dogs, sniffing her mouth, justifiably think she wants to play, but Molly threatens fiercely.

At what would have been the time of birth, dogs who have had false pregnancies carry "puppy" things around to replace the puppies, to satisfy the mothering instinct. But Molly is not replacing puppies. She has them. She actually has as many puppies as she has toys, although I think the mathematical relationship might not have been on her mind. But it may have: a certain amount of many is equal to a certain amount of many. And I do know that crows can count to seven and one gorilla at the Toronto Zoo can count to four.

The garage, the yard, the kennel, the kitchen, are strewn with toys. Why these, why now?

Tasha, an exceptionally bright dog living in a family that worked hard to communicate with her—they howled with her and talked to her endlessly—did something similar. The family was dysfunctional. The mother, having drunk herself into oblivion, had finally left the two children and her husband. The dog became, not surprisingly, mother-caretaker. She was fierce about visitors. It was her home and she was alpha dog. When her little family left for a vacation without taking her along, she went to the teenage girl's room and pulled the doll collection from its shelves. Then—and she must have done this one at a time—she carefully laid out each doll on the lawn. What did she mean? What instinctual behavior was this? Was it instinctual? It hardly seemed so, it was so intentional and intellectual and emotional. The next time Tasha stayed at home with a caretaker, the dolls' having been made inaccessible to her, Tasha removed all of the girl's hair ribbons and laid them out on the lawn with the same precision that she had treated the dolls. The following family holiday came just after Christmas. This time, the house empty, Tasha took each of the figures (mother, father, baby, wisemen) from the créche under the tree and laid them out neatly on the lawn. Again one at a time, as purposefully as a mathematician. What was the equation? She missed her family?

Or was she stealing the precious babies that belonged to her family, enraged as she was because they'd left her? Or was she building her own family back into being, magically, because they were gone and she was distraught that they were without her protection? On the lawn, in her place, she knew where they were, she had them hidden in her den, and they were safe. Not until Molly started carrying her toys did I really think I had a clue to Tasha's behavior.

When our cat had kittens, her sister cat stole them and hid them under a bed in the guest room. I've seen footage of wild African dogs stealing litters from each other, carrying puppies away into their own dens. Dominant females fight over puppy ownership. I've watched the defeated mother, puppyless, grieving, pacing the space just outside the territory of the victorious female, the new mother. That would explain why Molly wouldn't let her daughters into the two rooms: the one that I'd set aside for the puppies, the adjoining one that she'd set aside for herself. One can no longer rely on the cover-up phrasing "instinct," "territory." There is more. Teddy, a Golden retriever, when left alone in the house for the first time, collected everyone's shoes, piled them in the living room, dragged two coats over the pile, and lay on what I now consider, and he might have considered, his substitute family. Teddy and Tasha created a new family. I am not surprised, then, at Molly's behavior.

It is an unusually warm winter day, and I set up an exercise pen on the front porch. I put Molly on the back porch so I can move her puppies without either of us challenging the other. I carry the puppies one by one and put them into the new pen, watch them sniff the cold air, huddle, then spread out to inspect this entirely new situation of sunshine, wind, and the shape of things. Molly, allowed on the front porch, startled to see her puppies in the pen, in the wrong place, not her place, but my place, races away and whips into the whelping room. There she runs from whelping room to sofa, back and forth, collects all of her puppy toys, piles them in a corner of the box, and runs outside to check on the real puppies. The toys—frog, Snoopy, shoe, hedgehog, hot dog—are her replacement puppies, but why?

Is it because I'm the alpha dog and she has to relinquish her natural control over her puppies? Indeed, I feed them, pick them up, hold them, carry them into the kitchen when I warm their formula. She can't make me stop touching them. They smell of me. Torn between her ancient dog instinct to keep them hidden and safe and her understanding that I can do with them what I want because she is basically without power in my presence, torn between instinct and the learned, she exercises her ancient instincts in a way safe for us both. She exercises her double nature, integrates the instinct of the wild with the hierarchy of the household. She transfers her feelings to the inanimate. She collects another set of puppies just in case I take her own because having me take her puppies is painful to her. Perhaps she is also forgiving me, not attacking me. Molly is working toward becoming a different sort of dog in that endless, uneasy shift and struggle between dog and human.

Molly, Teddy, and Tasha acted with feeling and planning. We are all driven by needs. Molly worked hers out as well as she could under the circumstances of being a civilized dog. Otherwise, less civilized, she would have hidden the puppies themselves in that soft spot under the basement stairs.

Not only had Molly established her own backup family; she

had, Ben discovered, established her own den. The sofa excites Ben. We hear loud sniffs, hear him jump onto the sofa. Molly flies from the whelping box into the living room and roars at Ben. Not able to defend herself against my authority, she simply stands by as I find tucked into the tufted suede sofa in the living room her collection of puppy toys, a roasted pig ear in the corner, and, in each depression made by buttons into the stuffed sofa, a careful deposit of two or three kernels of dried dog food. She had left no telltale slime, no sign that she herself had eaten anything on the sofa. Here is her cache. Behind the sofa, against the wall, I find a dozen cookies. Each deposit is, for me, a symbol of Molly's anxiety about her puppies' welfare. She crossed the line between her netherland of what can be done as a domesticated dog and what she needed to do. I feel a terrible guilt because I made her suffer, made her worry too much about her puppies, pushed her trust too far, forced her to share, and it has been difficult, emotionally difficult, to share her puppies with me.

❧

The pups are over a month old. Rosie and Silky will stay with us. We have found wonderful, loving owners for the other three, who will be old enough to start their lives as dogs in another month. They are all layered with fat and fur, resistant enough to chills so I can leave them on the back porch for longer periods. For days, while the puppies play on the back porch, Pippa lies on a snowbank, watching them at a safe distance from Molly. Molly will not allow Pippa to approach the puppies but will allow the puppies to approach Pippa. Pippa licks their faces and they hers. She rolls over for them and lets them climb the mountain of her belly and spill down her back. One afternoon Molly fastidiously and pointedly looks away, away from her pups, away from Pippa, stands, walks past Pippa, leaves the porch. The puppies follow but reach Pippa first. Molly continues along the snowy path, leaves Pippa, clearly, very clearly, alone with the puppies. Molly's nipples hurt; she's been through a great deal. She's recovered from her pregnancy. She wants to play. She goes into the woods to check on her secrets. It is now Pippa who takes the puppies for short walks on the snowy lawn, demonstrates with great exaggeration the invitation-to-play bow, invites them to nip and roll on her, leads them into the woods, shows them the game of chase and take-away. Pippa now has puppies to play with: Molly has quit her job. But then Pippa takes aunthood a step further; she picks up Molly's puppy toys and walks around with them hidden in her great mouth. Molly has allowed Pippa to have both families of puppies: the real and not so real.

The birth of a litter is a time of celebration. When Molly had her last litter almost two years ago, the house was filled with visiting breeders, friends with young children, endless rounds of tea and cookies. Because that litter was sired by a Topmast father, Champion Cayuga's Icebreaker of Topmast, a world-class Newfy with championships in many countries, because Molly is basically a Topmast female, many breeders and two nationally known trainers, as well as friends and Newfy aficionados, came to see the litter. It was an exciting time. Only three thousand Newfies are born each year. Very few of them are Landseers, fewer still Topmast Landseers.

Each visitor chose Pippa as the "keeper"—the word they use for the one to keep. What was it the breeders saw in Pippa? "Show me," I would ask.

"Alertness. An animated curiosity, lively, vital. Her bone is big. See the relationship of the jawbone to the dome of the head? See how big her feet are? The distance from the tip of the nose to the stop [the point at which the forehead begins] should be half of the distance from the stop to the occipital bone [a strong pointed bone in the center of the skull]. See, her head is nearly perfect. The distance between the eyes should be about the width of the muzzle. See?" They'd tell me more: "Feel the muscling in the rear, the set of the ears, the thickness at the top of the tail. Put your fingers between her front legs. See how wide her chest is?" The trainers explained that they came to see the puppies because Topmast dogs are better than most others for search and rescue work. "When others quit," they said, "the Topmast dogs persevere."

Pippa's tiny crocheted collar was bright red against the flashy shoulder piece—the white gleaming ruff below her neck that runs to her saddle. Her nose had a blaze, a white stripe going up to her forehead. Her ears were velvet, her eyes dark and round. She was the first one to lift her head over the whelping box and look around. I kept music on in the whelping room. With their soothing hymns the Christian stations were the best. But one day I happened to be in the room and heard the opening notes of *Bolero*. Pippa heard them also. I hadn't realized the puppies were already able to hear. Pippa lifted her little head, walked, wobbled over to the source of the sound, cocked her ears, this side, that side, back and forth, and heard music. Pippa was the name of a little girl in a Browning play who sang "Morning's at seven; . . . / God's in his heaven— / All's right with the world." Pippa's registered American Kennel Club name is Blue Heaven's

Morning's at Seven. It was a name that fit from the moment she opened her eyes.

It wasn't the specific measurements that convinced me to keep Pippa. I loved the way she looked. There was something Greek here, something that sang of the forms of athletes. There was harmony and power. There might be performance. At eight weeks a magic window opens through which puppies look in miniature what they will look like matured. A week earlier, a week later, the image is gone. The puppy is the plan. The ratios of the mature body will ultimately be the same as the ratios at eight weeks. Humans change their ratios from infant to adult. The placement of our belly buttons shifts and remains shifted. But in a mature Newfy the ratios return. Margaret Willmott, the owner of Topmast Kennels, told me, "If you have a good puppy, be patient. You'll have a good dog." For as many breeders who believe this, there are as many who disagree. Yet just this week I went to baby-sit for a day-old litter. The breeder, who had been breeding Newfs for twenty-five years, said, just before she went off to close her eyes after twelve hours of whelping and helping, "Pick out a girl and a boy." Indeed, I chose exactly the girl and the boy she had. We don't know what we see but we do see something. Between that first moment of intuition and the final moment where you can make a true judgment, there is a period when the pups, from six months old until two years, get the "uglies." The body grows too long for the legs, the head too small for the body, the rear too high in the air for the front, the topline—the straight line from shoulder to tail—seesaws from week to week, and their legs seem to go in different directions when they move. Even though they look as if rubber bands, not sinew, hold them together, the pattern is still imprinted. Barring bad nutrition, illness, and accident—falls, twists, breaks, chips, slams—the pup will attain that original graceful crystalline idea of form glimpsed at the eight-week window. Finally your Newfy elongates, fills out, thickens. The chest drops, the head swells, the legs angulate correctly. After the bitch has been in season—"in heat," as we say—you notice one day that she is in balance, sexy, confident, full, lovely, graceful, together. Everything works as it did when she was a puppy. One day the male suddenly stacks himself, legs slightly apart, neck stretched forward, back straight, head high, standing to attract a female, and there he is, full grown and wonderful, a work of art. And this is what I expected of Pippa, what the visiting breeders who looked in the whelping box predicted. So we kept her, and in her first winter she splayed out on ice and chipped both elbows. For months, for years, she couldn't move well, was sluggish and in pain. I rarely trained her. Finally, after hours of acupuncture, veterinary chiropractics, and just growing, Pippa, at two and a half years, is back to her puppy perfection.

⌘

Pippa has become a serene and mysterious bitch, a big silent, sultry, luxurious bitch. She's built wider and stronger than my other females, as powerful and huge as a male, larger than Ben, smaller than Toby, far larger than her mother, Molly. Pippa's sister, Dunya, who lives in the Lake Tahoe area with the woman who bred Molly, had eleven healthy pups for her first litter. I'm sure, when we do breed Pippa with some Newfoundland prince, she will be as fertile and productive. She is built to rescue men from heaving seas, pull foundering boats to shore, procreate.

Her fur is sleek and thick, silvery white all over with black markings: head, saddle, and buns. She has too much ticking—little black spots in the white fur—for perfection, according to the Newfy judging standard, and her tail is too long, although gorgeous in its plumed sweep. Pippa is a water dog, a working dog, a serious dog. Her head has become a massive domed triangle of deep-napped velvet, commanding, extraordinarily handsome. Round, glistening coal black eyes are set between overblown Tartar cheekbones. Her eyes are the saddest, most sympathetic eyes I've ever looked into. Below those eyes, projecting from her very serious solid black head, Pippa sports a great white freckled nose that makes the massive triangle comic, a clown's face with all the heartbreak at one end and the silliness at the other. The silliness is compounded by white whiskers, which are in a constant state of pleasure: curled upward toward the nose. I've never seen her whiskers droop sorrowfully. I've never heard her whine. She rarely barks.

Pippa seems cast from another mold, an older mold. I'm certain Pippa carries a good bundle of wild genes, instincts, and actions built into her system long before domestication. She carries, it seems, more than my other dogs. Wild dogs have larger brains, I've heard, lose one-sixth of their brainpower in domestication. I think Pippa has kept whatever it is domesticated dogs have lost. She's more adult than they are, more distant, more of a hunter, more private, more of an individual. I think of Pippa in a wilderness. When she looks out over a horizon, scanning it in a way that sends shivers up my spine, I ask her if she remembers a wild shoreline, waves crashing, the shriek of heaving seas, men overboard, saving them. She might remember.

When all the other dogs are banging at the back door to

come into the sanctuary of the warm kitchen, Pippa remains on the lawn, inviting snow and wind, her long white fur ruffled by the arctic winds screaming in from her past lives. Pippa is so quiet, so unwilling to express pain, fear, tension, hunger. She is very much like my middle child: a brilliant, proud, and private distant child who never disobeyed but wrote her true feelings in her diary. If Pippa had fingers, she might keep a diary. When Pippa sleeps with me at night, she sleeps at the far end of the bed. Because I know she likes the fresh air, I leave the doors to the balcony open in the summer and a window wide open in winter, although I then wear a hat and a scarf and hide under my comforter. There are some winter nights when we wake up with snow on the floor. Pippa doesn't come close to me on the bed unless I call her. When I stop petting her and playing in her fur, she moves away again to the far end of the bed. Sleep is very important to Pippa. When disturbed—I can't keep my hands from her fur—her tail flops against the floor or the mattress in polite, limited acknowledgment. No other parts move. Her eyes don't open. She is very clear about the necessity of sleep. In contrast with Ben's hair-trigger reactions to my least motion, Pippa sleeps until she wakes, not until I wake. Her grunts wake me. In the morning I invariably find her on the floor in front of the French doors doing her upside-down wake-up stretches. She is, as far as I can judge, neither awake nor asleep. She is on her back, all four legs up in the air, running through time and space. In her dreamtime, in her wilderness, where limbs don't falter and breath doesn't run out and elbows don't chip on the ice, she chases wild beasts, growls, barks, all upside-down. Earth isn't involved. Gravity is nonexistent. Perhaps it feels like flight.

Sometimes I have seen her on her back, trotting, opposite legs moving; sometimes I have seen her galloping, her two front legs kicking forward as if she's leaping across terrain. Oh, Pippa, who are you? How miraculous that you've come bounding from the eternity of the wild to live with us for our short moments, to love us, for we are nothing to your mysteries. I kneel next to her and touch her with my reality. Her eyes open. She wags her entire upside-down self and invites me to come down to her. And I nuzzle my head into the soft long hairs of her neck. We could knit cashmere scarves with that neck hair. Her tail—too long, that tail—is a sweeping plume for a king's horse. Megabitch, Pippa, sports eleven nipples, three more than the standard.

I take her great head in my hands and lift the powerful jaws. She looks into my eyes. She does not waver. We drink each other in like lovers. Her head is a bucket of mute sadness, so sad, so kind, so sympathetic, one melts. I scratch her chest, rubbing, scratching, deep in the muscular recesses under her collarbone. She looks up into a place of pleasure above her, to the right, stretches her body so that I'll move my hand into another crevice, another pleasure spot. People look to that point above themselves, to the right, when they are trying to remember something. I wonder if Pippa is remembering something.

Of the quiet dogs, she is the most quiet. If the others are begging for a bit of my breakfast muffin, circling my knees, thumping their rears on the floor to make certain I know they are sitting, Pippa will sit away from the table and wait for me to invite her. She offers no thumping, no demonstrations, no demands. We often put her on a diet before shows. Her 120 pounds, which look athletically correct on Ishtar and Molly, look fat on Pippa because of her wide, seaworthy berth. The other dogs eat six cups of dry food a day. Pip is allowed only two cups of dog food and two cups of vegetables, and I know she's very hungry. Yet she is too proud to approach and beg. She simply stares at me, waits for eye contact. When I offer her food, she takes it gently, lifting the side of her soft, jowly mouth, with exquisite manners. Of all the dogs, she has the softest mouth. She takes food from the side without frontal snapping. One night we discovered she had another method of taking food. Dieting, she was not losing weight. Her belly was round and fat, basketball hard. Where was she getting food? Then we saw her body-slamming the freezer. A box of dog biscuits sat on top of the freezer, set on its side so I could reach into it easily. She had found that by body slamming the freezer, she could shake down a cookie, lots of cookies, all the cookies.

Pippa is the only dog I've had who looks to the sky. I have come across her in the woods, sitting beneath a tall white pine, looking high up into its branches. The others might run and dash around a tree that holds a cheeky squirrel or a dangerous raccoon, but they won't look up. It is as if Pippa had been born with a set of experiences my other dogs don't carry. After we've played water games and everyone is cavorting, charging around the lawn, shaking, and leaping, Pippa will sit in the water, as solemn, as sad as an orphan, seeming to say she wants to play more. She wants me to come out into the water. She sits waiting silently with her long, heartbreak face, sits and watches. Sometimes I'll give in and throw four or five more sticks. Still she sits and waits. Swimming and retrieving the stick isn't play for her.

Her blood, I know, surges to jump overboard and rescue men, logs, ropes. Early in this century, Landseers were caged at the docks in Halifax for fishermen to rent for the day. Pippa's blood is very old. She shakes off her veils of water and follows me up the lawn.

Perhaps Pippa is more mysterious than the others because she grew up alone, a middle sister who couldn't roughhouse, a child who behaved but remained distant. Her two years were framed by my husband's cancer operation and then my own. We had little time or energy for training, for developing a one-on-one intimacy. She became a well-behaved dog because the other dogs were. When we walked to new places, she watched Ben, not me. She did whatever he did, took his left, right, his pause. If there was a choice of directions, she checked to see what he was doing. In the stream, out of the stream, across the bridge, stop, start. She was happy with her dog family, friendly and pleasant and obedient to us.

So Pippa just grew and grew and became actually indelicate, a moose, loose, wide, and lumbering, a body slammer. I've seen her race up the lawn, charging after, alongside, then neck to neck, position herself perfectly, and slam bang Toby with her rear end, toppling him, just the way she slammed the freezer to shake down some cookies. We exulted in her power, her size, and her good nature. She was not a smooth dog, not athletic. We didn't take her seriously, nor she us.

As part of the program to smooth Pippa's movement, I took her to an itinerant veterinary chiropractor. Pippa had limped so much on one leg for so many reasons, I was certain she'd thrown her hip out, and indeed she had. The chiropractor was seeing her dog patients in a turn-of-the-century summer cottage by a lake. Other dogs and owners stood around watching the chiropractor work. Pippa watched very carefully. Then I brought Pippa forward. The chiropractor, at that moment an angry woman—there was some issue about getting lunch—sat on the floor, giving directions to her assistant in what may have sounded like snaps and hisses. When Pippa enters a new room, she lies down on the floor next to a piece of furniture, ideally the one I'm on. But this time Pippa climbed onto the one sofa in the room from which she could look down on the chiropractor, who certainly seemed to be bristling. She climbed up in order to look down, to dominate, to make certain the dangerous woman giving off bad vibes on the floor knew just who Pippa was. And indeed, to the chiropractor's great credit, she knew Pippa's self-image was such that she felt entitled to respect. The chiropractor gave it to her. She didn't stand. She spoke directly to her from the floor, softly, said, "Well, you really are a queen, aren't you?" And then, after a few moments, very politely, with no sarcasm in her voice, she asked Pippa if she'd mind coming down to the floor so she could work on her bones. Pippa jumped right down, put her nose to the vet's nose, and agreed. It was a perfect demonstration of Pippa's nobility. Other breeders in the room remarked, "She's letting the vet know just who she is." There was no fawning, no whining, no backing away, or stubbornness. It was not quite "Hurt me and I'll rip you limb from limb," but it was clear Pippa was in control of the situation, far more so than the vet.

Pippa works to act correctly in new situations. I find her

adaptability extremely sophisticated. Pippa's sister Bear With Me came to visit at six or seven months. Something had gone wrong for Bear With Me. She was unsocialized. Although she'd grown up in our house, run up and down the hall she had just entered, she was very frightened. Pippa sniffed her, recognized her as her litter mate, joyously leaped and jumped around her. But Bear With Me cowered at her owner's ankles. Pippa approached more slowly, dropped into a play bow. Bear With Me didn't respond. Bear With Me sat at her owner's feet. Pippa sat in front of her. Bear With Me looked away. Pippa rolled over on her back to show submission. "Look, don't be afraid." Bear With Me couldn't respond. Pippa tried again and again to bring Bear With Me out from under her owner's feet. Bear With Me didn't have the courage. It wasn't, I'm certain, because she'd been abused in any way. Her owners were wild for her. But something had gone wrong. It could have been the large, aggressive dog they already owned; it could have been she needed more socialization, more trips to supermarkets and malls, new places, new people. She had no confidence, and I didn't know why. I don't think she had been hurt, unless the large dog had pounded her or frightened her. Newfs are extremely forgiving but overwhelmingly sensitive.

Pippa ran up and down the hall, resting again in front of Bear With Me. We watched Pippa work a mad muscular repertoire of friendship, invitation, mimicry. A grand and generous soul, Pippa continued to adjust her behavior to Bear With Me's needs. Finally, with Bear With Me lying at her owner's feet, Pippa stretched out and lay in front of her, doing, it seemed, whatever it was Bear With Me wanted to do as long as they were doing it together. Bear With Me's fear broke my heart. I wanted to bundle her into my arms and love her. I couldn't. I had sold her.

Had they not loved her enough? Left her alone too long? Exposed her to too many frightening situations? Were her owners heavy-handed with her? Did they fight with each other and frighten her? Was she afraid of the other dog? Bear With Me was not happy and, for very good reasons, the owners were not happy. Eventually the owners decided to put her to sleep because they were moving to an apartment. The night before she was to be put down, I heard about it. I called the vet's office and found another home for her. Whether her confidence came from maturity or change of place, I don't know, but Bear With Me today is well, happy, and, unfortunately, very fat—clearly living the good life surrounded by horses on seventy fenced acres.

One of the subtle competitions among breeders is, not how much we sold a puppy for, but how many fenced acres he will have. It is difficult to express the fury in my heart when one of my puppies doesn't work out. After every litter I want to keep them all. When buyers sign contracts, I say I want the key to their front door. It's a joke, but I mean it.

❧

Because Pippa is so big, strong, and undemanding, so silent, I had assumed she was uncomplicated and confident. I found out quite otherwise when I entered her in a large show in Michigan. She had seemed so lovely and her movement seemed so smooth, I thought she was ready to compete. En route she traveled well, slept well, ate well, seemed as confident as she had at home and at smaller shows. But she fell apart in this show. On the first day, standing as the judge examined her, she looked gorgeous and highly competitive, but as soon as she moved, she dragged, limped, and lumped around the ring. The judge ignored her. "She is such a beautiful bitch," a sympathetic handler said, "but she's in pain." She didn't seem to be in pain outside the ring. At dawn of the next day when I walked her around the grounds of the show site, she sprang about, invited every Newfy she met to play. All she wanted to do was course and crash through the paths of an adjacent cherry orchard. The blossoms were just opening. The new sun played on glistening petals and on her silken fur and on the underside of wheeling gulls, all the iridescent energy of the dawn. It was that moment I'd been waiting for since I'd chosen her from the whelping box. The promise had been kept, the crystalline form shimmered. She was beautiful. She was breathtaking. Against my better judgment, I let her off the lead to race away from me. I didn't know if other dogs were exercising in the area. She burst through the geometries of the cherry orchard, here, there, gone, her footprints so strong on the dew, glorious; the joyous promise of that red-collared puppy looking around from her whelping box was fulfilled.

Aah, Pippa, why then did you limp in the ring? The limp was gone by the time we had driven home from Michigan, gone until the next show months later in Connecticut. She'd jumped into the van perfectly sound. She came out of the van limping on a rear leg, a new limp. A handler told me she had a Lhasa who limped only at shows. The little Lhasa's muscles tightened up because she was nervous. One thinks of little dogs as high-strung and nervous, but not big solid creatures like Pippa. I squeezed four drops of Dr. Bach's Rescue Remedy under her tongue to stabilize her. Yes, it's a strange elixir of flowers. Yes, no one knows how it works. Yes, it works. Our vet uses it on newborns, surgery patients, trauma patients. It works. In twenty minutes Pippa had lost her limp. I was so ashamed that I hadn't guessed; if she had told me in some way, I hadn't heard. This utterly reserved girl, a lady now, was nervous. I had paid little attention to her needs.

Pippa, my wild Diana, hunts daily. There is a dead tree with an open trunk. It is Pippa, I am certain, who has torn off wide swaths of bark high on the trunk, hunting as a bear would. Clearly some small creatures have taken refuge in the tree. Closer to home, a chipmunk who has discovered our garage, the bags of food, the spilled bits of crackers, and grows fatter each year, or has very fat children, is Pippa's goal in life. This chipmunk has survived my dogs by hiding in an old rain gutter laid behind the kennel area. Pippa hunts him daily, digs enormous holes, two and three feet deep, searching for him. I remember what the visiting trainers said about Topmast dogs being the best search and rescue dogs. I don't know if Pippa is planning rescue. She is certainly serious about the search. Others join her to help dig the holes or bark at either end of the rain gutter, but they drift away. Still, Pippa works at finding that chipmunk. In the house she is as assiduous about the cat—poor cat, who has learned to count Newfoundlands. I think she may count Pippa twice. Pippa has tried and failed to adapt to the cat. The cat is not flexible in any way. She is able only to be a cat. Pippa's first duty on entering the house is to run upstairs and find the cat. The cat will hiss, growl, and claw from my husband's desk, from under a bed. The cat knows the dog's reach, knows the safe places. At night, the cat hiding, sort of, under my bed, Pippa lies in front of the dust ruffle, the cat temptingly just behind the dust ruffle. Pippa wags her tail in a hard, firm, happy tempo. "Do you want to play? Do you want to run? I'll chase you." The cat wants to fight. Pippa, who makes, at the most, two or three sounds a month, whines a begging whine, which is the same sound Ben makes when he means "please": a small, high-pitched, non-threatening infant sound. Molly, trying to convince her puppies to play with her, has made this same high "please" squeak as if she is—and isn't she?—talking baby talk. Beneath the bed, Pippa talks baby talk to the cat, harmless, singing sounds that mean "I won't hurt you." She is not hunting. She wants to play. What she is doing with the invisible chipmunk, the creatures who dwell in the tree trunk, I don't know. I do know she is as determined to play with the cat as she was to play with her sister Bear With Me. Pippa must have taken a hit from the cat. She comes up on the bed and licks her nose. She stretches out, but she can't sleep. Down she goes to try to convince the cat, yet again, that friendship with a Newfoundland is safe. I firmly believe if she were to corner the cat, she would not hurt it, but Pippa might get hurt. The cat is unable to change its evolutionary package.

What I think has allowed our dogs to evolve into the sympathetic beings we can live with, and in some ways beings very much like ourselves, is their adaptability, their willingness to lead our lives. Some friends had a Newfy named Sarah. They called her Sarah the Centerpiece. Each evening, at dinnertime, Sarah climbed up onto the center of the table and stretched out.

"If I can't sit on a chair as they do, certainly I can lie on the table. That's almost what they are doing." The family ate around her. She watched. Sarah never begged, never took anything. She didn't know how to sit on a chair. She did know how to lie down. Lying on the table was as close as she could be with her family, as near as she could come to doing what they did. It was a big table. It isn't beyond me to consider the idea that Sarah was moving in as close to the food as she might, but still, she didn't take anything or make a begging fool of herself, and I read her behavior as polite and very dear. It also takes a very special family to live with this kind of centerpiece.

⚬∞⚬

The sequence of events every morning begins with a walk around the entire yard, and then everyone goes into the kennel to wait for breakfast. They file in, reluctantly, and they take their places on the wooden deck at the front of the kennel or choose one of the four doghouses lined up facing the deck. Entering the kennel means getting a bone, a cookie, or a pig's ear. Because this sequence is what we taught Ben and Molly and repeated over and over again every morning, it was easily imprinted on all young dogs. One day Pippa broke the sequence with a charade, planned and specific. I closed the kennel gate. Everyone settled down and I turned around to see Pippa, sitting pointedly, symbolically, not quite hiding, hardly hidden, behind a slender maple tree. She had approached the kennel as I had asked her, doing whatever the pack was doing. But this day she was telling me she really didn't want to go in. Certainly she knew I could see her. She was only eight or ten feet away from me. She had a clear idea of the distance she needed to keep to be out of my control. She had made the approach, hadn't run away, just sat there watching me, trying to establish eye contact. It was our first true communication. She told me she really didn't want to go into the kennel, that she understood, that she was a good girl, but she would not like to go in. She had expressed a need, and her need was, at last, to be with me. I walked over to her, put my hand on her head, not in control, more in benediction, told her that I understood her feelings, but she had to go into the kennel. I put my hand on her collar. It wasn't necessary. She stood and followed me docilely to the kennel gate, entered, sat with the other dogs. I didn't give her a cookie. Then, because she needed to know I was listening to her, I let her out and brought her into the kitchen, gave her the cookie, and spent the afternoon with her, allowing her to lick pots and pans and get snacks and a brushing. She wanted to be a house dog. This lovely Pippa had been waiting. We'd made a breakthrough.

I had to be very alert to what might be inattention, rebellion, or genuine expression. There was such a thin line between expressing herself and misbehaving. We walked it. I had to work with Pippa.

Now that she knew I listened to her, the messages began. At night the younger dogs sleep in the garage. Before we go to bed, we let them out to relieve themselves. Like zombies, they file out the garage door to the lawn, lift a leg or crouch, walk back in, flop in their blanket nests, and go back to sleep. One winter night, Pippa, instead of returning to the garage as usual, took another turn and climbed the steps toward the kitchen. Hers was a new message, clear and precise: "I want to be with you. I want to sleep inside with you."

Pippa is mature now, and part of that maturity is the silent constant message that she belongs inside and belongs with me. She is no longer a puppy to be treated lightly. Now Pippa travels to shows, and she knows what to do. She is completely attentive to my movements. When we check into a motel, she waits for me to put a pail of fresh water in the bathroom, and then lies down next to the bed, watches me, follows me, acts as she thinks I want her to act. She has become my dog. Or I am her dog. Or we are each other's dogs. It took almost a year and a half for us to bond. When she approaches my place, my seat, my bed, she cautiously licks the corners of my mouth, a dry little lick, as if she doesn't dare express what she feels, certainly less passionate a lick than I get from the others, but a lick nonetheless, a recognition of my place and her place and her place with me. Now and then, when there are no other dogs around, she will allow herself to groom me. One night she did my entire right arm, fingers to shoulder. My husband had taken over the puppy watch, and I was, to say the least, passive, having flung myself into the bed. I was almost asleep. Perhaps that's why Pippa felt she could really love me—when I wasn't watching. I remembered how she had waited for Molly's puppies to come to her, that she had not dared approach them but lay on the snowbank near them while they played around their mother. And then one day a puppy came over, and the others followed. From that moment on, they were her puppies. Pippa had waited until no one was looking and then loved. She had waited for the puppies and I think she had been waiting for me. She must have known when I was ready. I know she has perhaps come a longer way to love and be loved than the others. She has sacrificed her wilderness to allow herself to love.

Pippa, thank God, has not had the opportunity to do anything heroic. She'll stand still for me and hold her ground if I need to balance myself going down a slippery hill. She'll let the new puppies ride on her back when she's swimming. She'll lick me when I fall. I am certain, if anything is needed from Pippa, she will be there for me. These are not simple souls, these Newfies. We owners joke with each other that our Newfies are not dogs. It isn't such a joke. A recent story tells of a Topmast relative of Pippa's, a Newfy puppy raised with a Rottweiler puppy. They did everything together, and were, as only puppies can be, inseparable. One day when they were both nine months old, watching traffic from the front porch, a newspaper boy came by on his bicycle. The boy did something that offended, alarmed, threatened the Rottweiler, who leaped off the porch and threw the paper boy to the ground. The Rottweiler, whose instinctive character is that of a killer guard dog, held the boy to the ground and went for his throat. The Newfy pup leaped on the Rottweiler and killed him. It is a story that reverberates with what we all know: The Newfy doesn't think he's a dog. His loyalty is to humans.

Perhaps their instinct to help us is as long-standing and ingrained as our instinct to trust them. Tuck, a great male, sat on the beach with his owners. Children asked permission to pat him. A little girl simply threw her arms around him, buried her head in his neck and cried. Perhaps we really did know each other well a long, long time ago. Allen Ransome, who sold me Ben and Molly, lives with Champion Walden Pond Ye Gads Indy, Toby's half brother, a huge male, in New York City. Tough, sophisticated city dwellers who ordinarily wouldn't meet each other's eyes fall on their knees to hug and love Indy. What instinct, what old connection, exists in us that so responds to them? Everyone smiles when they see a Newf. What is it, we keep asking ourselves, that they do for us?

I received an inkling from a young autistic boy whose vision of what Pippa could do for him in his terrifying world was clear and simple. I had taken Pippa, along with other Newfs, to a school for learning-disabled children. The boy was crouching under a desk but must have recognized something in Pippa he needed desperately, for he sprang from under the desk, ran to her, and flung himself under the roof of her belly. I thought about the well-dressed New Yorkers falling to their knees on the dirty sidewalks. Pippa gracefully moved away. She didn't wish to be dominant. He ran after her, threw himself under her again and yet again. Was it shelter he had recognized, the great sheltering ability of this creature? *"God's in his heaven— / All's right with the world"?* That poor, troubled little boy wanted only to lie under her, under the roof of her belly, within the columns of her legs. Perhaps that is why Pippa scans the horizon, watches for storms. Perhaps it is her duty to search for us, to rescue us, to shelter us. I hope she never has to, but I am very certain she would.

At four, Toby is breathtaking. He is huge, beautifully proportioned, with a great glossy coat, voluminous britches on his rear legs, and long silken furnishings on his front. His tail is thick and powerful. He is altogether what a male Newf should be. He is more impressive than Ben, but sillier and very soft, as breeders would say, a mush of a personality. He has a funny, sweet look about him, something clownish that reminds everyone of Chewbacca in *Star Wars*. His hair parts up the middle from forehead to crown like that of a 1930s film star. Through his mother, Mariah, he's a cousin to Ben and Molly.

When I first saw Toby he was a few hours old. Eight weeks later he was a young fat tank of a puppy with dark glistening eyes, entirely black except for a tiny white flag on his chest. I knew his father, Raven's Cove Waterlord, who was magnificent, and his mother, Walden Pond Mariah, who was pretty and painfully shy. Toby was sold to a man who already had two Newfs. Three were too many. He sold Toby at ten months to a young family who kept him for three days and called the breeder. Poor Toby. Because he'd been ignored, he didn't know how to behave. Because he didn't know how to behave, he would be ignored, unloved, without the home a Newf deserves. It wasn't his fault.

Although the new buyer must have known that keeping a big untrained dog in a family with young kids is courting disaster, he couldn't resist Toby and brought him home, but Toby didn't fit this family at all. So the husband tied him to an apple tree and called the breeder, who called me to look at Toby.

I drove to the new owner's home the same day I heard about Toby. He was, after all, family. He was potentially of show and breed quality, not pet quality. And he deserved a better life. The slight young wife was eight months pregnant and had a two-year-old daughter. In his enthusiasm and need for love, poor Toby had knocked over the wife and child the first day. Mother and child were sitting tight-lipped on lawn chairs, watching Toby as he ran around the apple tree in agitated circles, tying himself up tighter and tighter.

Toby was quite wonderful. His paws were saucers and his head was huge. Although narrow and immature, he had the promise of power, size, and the show quality of his father. I called my friend Hannah, a fellow breeder. She drove over. We decided to buy him together. But it wasn't that simple. The young husband wanted to make certain Toby was going to a good home. So we invited him over to a puppy class in which, that night, that idyllic night, ten Newfs were training on the lawn with their owners. Toby watched. When training was over and the dogs were freed to dash into the lake to swim, Toby jumped in, galloped through the water, raced with the other Newfies up the lawn. He had to be in heaven to be back with other Newfies, to be with a crowd of people. We had passed. Hannah and I bought Toby. He would live with me.

Toby was ten months old when he came to us, all leg, bone, very tall, very narrow, already powerful, with a particularly handsome head and deep soft eyes. He was already so high at the shoulder, when he walked under the kitchen table it lifted and moved along with him as we juggled cups and grabbed saucers. Although he showed nothing abnormal on X-rays, his front movement was awkward. His toes turned in when he walked, and there was a funny paddle movement in the front legs. He had had some kind of accident.

I owned Molly and Ben and their puppies Celeste and Ishtar. I didn't need another dog. Toby was the beginning of my acquisition lust. He would be my stud dog; he would support the kennel. Well, I was a newcomer. What did I know? Nothing supports a kennel. Toby had had no training. He knew his name. He did not know what a leash was, and he weighed 120 pounds. Since a grown Newf can pull up to 3,000 pounds, Toby was, to say the least, not soft at the end of a lead. He knew no boundaries. The only positive aspects of his behavior were that he was loving, did his morning rituals in the woods, not on the lawn like everyone but Molly, and deferred carefully to the other dogs. Molly was sharp with him, lifted her bitch nose, exposed her fangs, and went after him. Toby backed away from her. Ben watched him carefully, stood between him and the puppies, between him and Molly, between him and me. Ben let him know that he owned the family and the territory. Toby paid respects to Ben by licking his lips and lying next to him.

We discovered quickly that Toby was a party animal. The first weekend I took him to the Newfoundland Club picnic at a lakeside park not five hundred feet from our house. One property—the original carriage house—lies between my house and the park, but I drove the short distance so Toby wouldn't know about walking there by himself. Toby was too wild, too curious, too excited for me to handle at the picnic, so I packed him in the car and drove him home to kennel him. As I let him out of the car, he took off, looked over his shoulder at me once (inviting or defying me), and raced down the lawn to the lakefront, back to the Newfoundland picnic. I arrived at the picnic grounds as he came up from the water, wet to his shoulders. There, in front of everyone, I had to pick up my prize by his jowls, yell, shake, and shame him. And myself. From then on, whenever there was a picnic, party, ball game, some sort of fun at the park, I would watch Toby carefully. Too often I found him, the very center of attention, surrounded by children hugging him, adults feeding him hot dogs.

Once and only once has anyone seen Toby swim again. He leaped into the water after a bitch in heat, swam out to her, swam back, and never, that I have witnessed, swam willingly again, although I have used a dozen methods to bring him out with me. Perhaps he thought I disciplined him up there at the picnic shoreline because swimming was a bad thing to do. He was being punished for something. How could he know he was being punished for running away? His last act had been swimming. He's happily been to many picnics since; he's happily taken his own excursions since; but never, except that once, have I seen him swim. I'm sure he thought he was being punished for swimming, decided that I was so unstable about his swimming, he'd just better avoid it altogether.

His training took priority over every other dog activity. In class Toby would sit pleasantly and then lose focus. We'd tap him on the head. "Earth to Toby. Earth to Toby." Toby had to acknowledge that we had something worth hearing. "Cookie." "Car." "Up." "Hungry." He'd pay attention a few seconds longer each time.

I think Toby had been confined all his young vital first puppy months. He was quiet in our house for the first few days, and then he burst, sprang, into activity. Like any teenager, he didn't know where he began and ended. He knocked over chairs, the contents of cupboards, the puppies. He meant no harm. When he first came to us we called him the dog from hell. His AKC name was Walden Pond Ramblin' Man, and he was. He also could have been called Houdini. He released himself from any confinement, leaving always as if he had serious business elsewhere. Keeping him with me was no easy proposition. I took him for walks on thirty-foot leads and whistled him back in for treats. I couldn't trust him off lead. But he eventually learned the whistle, and finally one day in a park I gave him freedom to go off lead. But though he'd learned the whistle, he simply had not learned to listen. It shouldn't have been a surprise, this inability to attend. No one had ever spoken to him, communicated with him, after he'd left the breeder's kennel.

So he had his own set of rules and regulations and didn't understand there could be other rules. When other rules were enforced—stay in the kennel, sit in the back of the car—Toby continued his agitated circling, the same circling around the apple tree I had seen the day I'd gone to meet him. Clearly he was stressed.

As the goddesses of myth who took the beasts to bed to civilize them, I decided that Toby would sleep in my room at night. In my bed at night. On the bed, off the bed. On the bed, off the bed. I would lie still, listening to him circling my room, circling, as agitated as he'd been under the apple tree, and then a big sigh and crash as he dropped to the floor to sleep. Again and again through the night, night after night, I would hear him circle, then crash. At last the time came when he slept through the night.

I lost a lot of shoes that week until I realized he was nervously working on them. To this day I wear shoes with his teeth marks on the heels. But that week Toby and I bonded, ever so slightly. He could not give me his soul as the others had, but he had at least learned to sleep through the night, that it was good to be with me, a privilege to be on the bed. He didn't know he had to be with me.

The mantra of our home was, "Where's Toby? Toby's loose—keep the doors closed." Toby simply took any exit he could find. The other dogs wouldn't dream of leaving. It was their job to be with me, perhaps their heart's desire. Not so with Toby. I began to put on fairly appropriate clothes early in the morning because running up and down the road through backyards in my nightgown was not in my image. I can remember running home through the woods, muttering, "I don't care. Get run over. I don't care." I cared terribly. Like an abandoned wife, a wraith in the mists of morning, I tramped the neighborhood, calling his name. I managed not to weep, but I was always terrified that beautiful Toby would be hurt. And there Toby would be, waiting for me on the correct side of the fence, on our property, somehow having found his way either through the water or up the road, and he would approach me with enormous hesitation because he knew something was out of sequence. It was his perception that I was on the wrong side of the fence, too far from the property. It was I who needed guidance and protection. He of course had gone for his walk without bothering anyone and returned and was where he ought to be. I wasn't. The rule is: Lift the bad dog by the jowls until his front feet are off the ground, then shake and yell and scream. Bad dog means a dog who doesn't come when called. Ready to pick him up as a disciplining mother bitch would, as Mariah must have, I would approach Toby, who would leap up and hug me and lick my face because I'd returned. What does one do with the fury?

I recall sitting at the lost child center at the New York State Fair, watching parents weep. As soon as the lost child was found, the weeping parents would yell and scream and hit. In desperation I called a friend who is an extraordinarily successful dog trainer. She came to play with Toby for a day. The first order of business was a walk around the boundaries of my property. Toby was wearing a pinch collar, a medievel torture affair with hooks that dig into the dog's neck if it's pulled. She walked Toby around and around the yard. He was delighted to walk with her and made no attempt to leave. So we cleverly devised a plan. I would stand in the woods beyond our boundaries and call Toby. She would jerk Toby back really hard so he associated pain and correction with crossing the boundary. Indeed, it worked. When Toby had been jerked back, he sat watching us with a "What next?" look on his big face. We congratulated him and let him free. He raced to the precise spot where his collar had been jerked, where he'd been corrected, and lifted his leg. "There. Marked. I won't make that mistake again." The house sits on five acres. There were thousands of spots Toby would have to mark, spot by spot. So we gave up and fenced the yard, leaving the only escape route at the lakefront. I had begun to assume Toby wouldn't swim again, that his escapes would be made only by land. He had never again reappeared wet.

If you call "Come" to a dog who is running away and he won't come to you, then he deserves his comeuppance and punishment and confinement in the run by himself. There is no worse punishment for a Newf than to be by himself. But if you find him on his way home, you certainly don't want to punish that behavior. He'll think it's bad to come home. I would always find him, visiting here or there, sniffing a new bush, rambling, heading toward home however slowly, however indirectly, but in the vague and correct direction. So I was rarely able to punish him. Reinforcing his return positively was much more important to the safety of the dog than punishing him for disobeying a "come."

The worst of Toby's escapes happened early one morning. The dogs sleep in the garage or, on warm nights, in the kennels. He wasn't in the garage or in his kennel. We jumped into the Suburban, aiming for Hannah's house, where Toby had bred a bitch the week before. Had he, in the early morning, testosterone running like sap, started out for Hannah's house five miles away? I didn't know how long he'd been gone. All night? Since morning? A half hour? And then, there he was, tongue hanging out to the side, lollygagging along the center line of the road that runs past our house. Cars and trucks looped carefully around him. Since he hated gravel under his footpads, he'd taken the macadam. Newfs are not afraid of cars. Cars mean new places, adventures, good, McDonald's, another Newf home, a show. Toby looked as if he'd covered a lot of territory. God knows what he was thinking. He was walking toward my house and was within a hundred feet or less of my driveway. I suspect his direction was home, home from somewhere, heading toward our house. He'd gone far beyond the park. Had he been looking for bitches in heat? Looking for the bacon someone was cooking up the road? Or just looking, making maps in his brain, rambling? I stopped the car. He poked his head in the window. I stepped out and attached a lead. He didn't need one. "Oh, thanks," he almost said. "I was getting tired." And he jumped into the back of the car. How could I punish him?

What I could do was close off his escape route, but where was it? At last, after furious searching, we finally found it, improbable though it was: a tiny paneless window in the rear of the old garage at the end of his kennel. We boarded up the window immediately. I still don't know how Toby fit his great self through that window frame.

As a puppy Toby had been ignored, so even though he knew his name, it meant very little to him. When he took off across a neighbor's property, no name-calling helped. He was of one mind and it was a dog mind. He would leave me. It wasn't as though he were left alone outside to wander. I would be walking with the dogs and suddenly Toby was off. If he was in the house and a screen door wasn't tightly closed, Toby was gone. He would always come back, and I'd find him, tongue out, panting, sitting on the front porch or in front of the kennel, close to the other dogs. He was willing to be a dog. He knew very little more than doghood. He had not yet had any experience as faithful companion.

Toby isn't bad. Perhaps he's been bored. He certainly isn't stupid. His curiosity seems to arouse his determination to see more than what our home offers, and I'm convinced that that curiosity is an outgrowth of his intelligence—indeed, that he is more intelligent than the rest of my dogs. It might be that he is so curious and so bright, no amount of "civilization"—of sit, come, stay, lie down—could change Toby. Obedience does not necessarily equate with intelligence. Animals with the largest brains and the greatest curiosity—whichever came first—are the ones who have wandered farther from the points of origin of their species. They are the ones who have filled their heads with maps. Toby was a mapmaker par excellence.

One crisp fall day on a trail next to a deep-cut stream, Hannah and I had eight dogs running. Almost at the beginning of the trail, Toby found a dessicated pheasant, lay down with it under a tree, and decided his hike was over. He would not come with us. I called and called and then went on ahead with the pack. We were a good quarter of a mile up the trail when Toby arrived, tongue out, steaming, without his pheasant. Hannah's Champion Ebunyzar's Promises to Keep, a very pretty big black bitch, took in his approach, understood that Toby had left his pheasant behind, and flew back down the trail. She was thinking, planning, certainly problem solving. A few minutes later she arrived with Toby's pheasant. It was an act of elegant precision. She had no time to wander, look around, search for the bird. She knew the trail, the place. She had mapped it precisely, imprinted that map in the recesses of her brain, and taken off the moment she knew Toby had abandoned the pheasant.

Since we take the same trail a few times a week, the dogs know it intimately and are aware of any change. The smallest limb fallen on the path is a momentous event and requires circling, sniffing, investigating in the extreme. For months I walked behind them, watching them explore, sniff the same place each time, examine the same log, the same bush for last spring's strawberries, the burrow hole from which a chipmunk had dashed four months before, the rock where Toby and Pippa discovered a box turtle. I realized that they make maps in their heads—scent maps, event maps, thing maps, texture maps, sequential maps—that much of their activity on the trails is mapmaking and map following. I know why Ben whines for me to open the car windows as we drive. His mapmaking needs the scent element. A ride in the car is mapmaking in the fast lane. New places, new smells, new maps, enlarge brains. The world is a newspaper. It is my world my dogs are mapping, my world they are imprinting. Now I pay attention to their world: the tree limb, the new hole, the crushed hay where the deer slept. I begin to read as they do. I am allowed, as I learn to pay attention, to participate, as my dogs do, in the wonders of the natural world, a world from which I had grown far apart.

The more curious an animal is, the farther he'll wander from his point of origin. The farther animals wander from their point of origin, the more maps they make, the larger their brains grow. Pet dogs do not mature to the extent wild dogs mature. They remain infantile in many ways, which of course allows them to live with us and accept us as ranking adults. Mapmaking is a juvenile trait driven by curiosity and fearlessness. Toby probably is the best mapmaker of them all. On the ferry to Edgartown, while the other dogs curled into balls in their crates, hiding from the strangeness and the changes in balance, probably a little seasick, Toby was up and at every window, watching the splash of the waves in a porthole, the trucks, cars, people. He had to see everything. It was his curiosity that allowed him to learn so much, to try so much, to wander and wonder so much. He was making maps in his head. Forgive me, Toby, you weren't running away from home; you were making maps of the neighborhood.

Toby is a creature of mixed instinct and high intelligence. When Toby is given a command that he doesn't wish to obey, he looks behind himself over his shoulder, his right shoulder. Is he still looking for a way out or imagining there's another dog behind him who should be obeying me, or is he looking back at, and longing for, his animal self? African natives claim that gorillas don't talk because if they did, we'd put them to work. Perhaps Toby won't listen because he wants his freedom. There are times when I give Toby the command to go into the kennel, and he looks over his shoulder, behind him. Annoyed, I repeat his name, forcing a happy tone as if going into the kennel were an exciting treat. "Oh, come on, Toby." Sooner or later, if I don't give up, he trots toward me, into the kennel, and lies down with the other dogs. One day I noticed him yawn while he was considering my command. I'd had that same response from Ben when he was growing up: a sign he was going to shift his behavior. Both boys, Toby and Ben, would yawn and then do what was requested. If Ben were doing something I didn't want him to do, I'd say, "Come," and he'd stop, yawn, and come to me. What did the yawn mean? It meant, for one thing, that Toby was listening after all, thinking about shifting his behavior, and then obeying. The yawn was always a signal of thought: She's asking me to do something.

Why do I yawn? To get more oxygen. Why does Toby yawn? Is he stimulating his brain? Perhaps bypassing his subcortical primitive brain and sending oxygen to his higher intelligence? Firing himself up to use his head rather than his instincts? Or just saving face?

Toby jumps on me only when I call the cat. When Toby is in the house and I lean out the front door to call the cat, Toby jumps on me. He jumps no other time. "Here, kitty, kitty, kitty." Toby arrives behind me, circles me awkwardly, performs strange hopping motions on his back feet, and finally leaps up on my back, hugs me from behind with his enormous paws, and tries to reach my face with his long tongue. I had no idea what prompted this. It wasn't until his original breeders came to see him that I understood what Toby was doing. Allen Ransome patted his own shoulders and said, "Toby, kissy, kissy." And Toby leaped up, hugged him, and kissed him. "Kitty, kitty" was close enough to "kissy, kissy" for Toby. Although I had changed the rules by turning my back to him, hence the awkward circle, Toby was trying desperately to give me the kiss I had requested.

Now I position myself firmly against trees, fences, doors, give Toby a straightforward frontal command for a kiss, and I get large sloppy wonderful frontal body hugs while he examines the world from an upright position.

Newfs are, of course, water dogs. Toby is not, whether through a lack of confidence, my own stupidity, or simply not liking water in his ears. I'll never know. Toby warily follows me to the shore but stretches out, nails himself to the earth, on the steps leading to the water. Now and then, if he is certain I won't force him in, he ventures out up to his belly. He loves riding on the front of the rowboat, and he makes an imposing prow ornament. But one day he saw a dog on shore, leaped from the boat, and sank like a boulder.

I tempt him with dog cookies that float in the water. I pull him into the water with a leash. I give him buoyancy by tying a lifesaver around his belly. Thinking he lacked confidence, I took Toby through two water-training courses and accomplished the requirements. He has swum alongside me, retrieved a rope, pulled a boat to shore, retrieved an object from under the water, and, to my great pleasure, rescued me by leaping into the water, swimming out to me, turning around me, and letting me hold his tail as he pulled me to shore. On shore he licked my mouth, eyes, and nose to make certain I could breathe. All water instincts are operational. Still, he will not swim unless I force him to swim. He jumps in as I pull the lead, swims around me, thrashes, and plows to shore. We took him to the beach in Edgartown. He despised the sand, ignored the ocean, loved the ferry, the cars, the trucks, the people, and, most particularly, the liquid manure in the field next to our cottage. Dog and my psychology aside, it may simply be that Toby won't swim because he hates water in his ears as much as he hates gravel and sand between his toes.

We can't trigger, or we have destroyed, Toby's water instinct, but he is more than willing to pull a cart as thousands of generations of Newfies have done before him. Newfs are working dogs and have been for centuries. They were part of the fabric of pre-industrialized England, making deliveries and hauling goods. In early America teams of Big Indian Dogs pulled logs from the forests. In 1804, when Lewis and Clark fitted out their expedition across the continent, they bought a Newf in Philadelphia for twenty dollars, which was a great deal of money then. The Big Indian Dog was a lifesaver and protector in the wilderness, a hunter, a carrier of goods. Modern Newfs take to cart pulling quickly. Toby, with his massive neck and shoulders, was a natural for drafting. We bought him a cart and a bright red harness.

I have no idea when something learned becomes an instinct, but I do know Toby took to cart work with the excitement and enthusiasm I wanted him to take to the water. Toby earned a title in pulling a cart and has a large bronze medal to hang around his neck. He learned to pull a cart forward and back up, learned "haw" and "gee," gave endless numbers of children steady rides on snow, on ice, on grass, willingly, and served as best man at my daughter's wedding by pulling an antique goat cart loaded with white gladioli down the aisle to the waiting judge. He and Ben pulled together, a perfect and obedient team. Ben was always uneasy about the cart unless he was hitched with Toby. Ben was being good about carting. Toby liked carting. At the wedding, both my gorgeous boys lay down in tandem at the side of the judge, watching the families and the bride and groom walk down the grassy aisle. Walden Pond Ramblin' Man Toby and Walden Pond Shore Acres Ben—a handsomer team of best men no one has ever had. And when Matron of Honor Molly came down the aisle by herself, wearing a little lace bonnet, and joined the boys at the judge's side, no matter what elements of family strife had erupted prior to the wedding, both sides laughed and, although perhaps less than delighted with each other, were delighted with the dogs.

We halfheartedly train the dogs to sit on the floor in a long stay while we eat our meal. I think sharing food is very important; so do they. It becomes, however, too disturbing, and we've limited them to table food at the end of the meal. But Toby has problems with waiting when there's butter on the table. Toby lies down, hops up, drops his head on the table, positions it next to the butter—it is always the butter—sighs over the butter. We correct him, and he lies down affably, remembers the butter, and hops up, puts his head on the table next to the butter. He must think we are awfully stupid not to understand what he wants. He certainly told us clearly and often enough. Once, though, the temptation being overwhelming, Toby thought through the problem of how to get the bread and butter. He did not lie down on command but left the room. We heard him rummaging around in the house, up and down the stairs, until he finally appeared with a treasure: a roasted pig ear. Roasted pig ears, which we order by the horrible hundreds, which often have the pig's number tattooed on them, which thank God do not have the pig's personal name tattooed on them, are a major long-lasting obviously delicious treat for the dogs. Toby is allowed to take one out of the box each day. He had obviously hidden this one. He laid it at my feet. Naturally Toby received a piece of bread with slabs of butter. Toby reasoned and came up with the idea of trade. It was an enormous stretching of the evolutionary envelope. I know there are trading rats. And I know at least one gorilla at the Lincoln Park Zoo in Chicago who trades stones for grapes. I've never had a trading dog before.

Toby demonstrated another sign of advanced thinking. The basic awareness test for great apes is measuring their reaction to their image in a mirror. Chalk is rubbed on the ape's nose while the ape is unconscious. The ape wakes up and looks in the mirror at his chalked nose. If he is a self-aware ape, he'll know the chalk doesn't belong and rub it from his real nose. He has seen his image and knows it has a dirty nose, knows that that image is himself and that his real nose must be dirty. He knows himself; he recognizes the image of himself. When Toby was two years old I took him to Washago, far above Toronto, to meet a lovely bitch. We stayed in a motel room with a wall mirror in the bathroom. Toby sat in the bathroom and watched me brush my teeth in the mirror. I touched his mirror nose with my toothbrush, made a soapy white mark on his mirror nose. He licked his real nose. I'd read the ape study on self-awareness. I touched his mirror nose again. Toby licked his real nose again. He knew the dog in the mirror was himself; he had recognized himself. We laugh when puppies growl and carry on at the puppy stranger in the mirror. The reflections are other. Toby had demonstrated what ape scientists call self-awareness: consciousness. These dogs are utterly and completely, fastidiously conscious of themselves, one another, and their humans.

What kind of dog is Ishtar's son, Buoy, that he offers cookies and toys to visiting dogs, dogs he doesn't know? Twice we have observed this extraordinary altruism. Near Thanksgiving, young Buoy, not a year long, came into his living room to find young Billy in a cage. His reaction to this new dog was to go to his own cage, rummage around among his treasures, and retrieve a large biscuit, which he dropped in front of Billy's cage, pushed it toward the cage with his nose, and backed away. Buoy's owners, whose family have had Newfies for three generations, had never seen anything like this. On Christmas, a son returned with his older Newf. The boys were separated from living and kitchen areas by a gate. Upon seeing the visiting Newf, Buoy once again ran to his cage, rummaged around, and brought out his new bright orange squeak toy, which he promptly dropped in front of the gate, pushed it toward the new dog and stepped back.

One of Toby's sons, Bosun, has shown the same ability to stretch the envelope of dog behavior. His six-year-old playmate taught him to climb the ladder of the playground slide and slip down. The sight of a great Newf hurtling down the slide is improbably wonderful. She also taught Bosun to play hide-and-seek. She hides and waits for him to find her. When he finds her, she says, "Boo!" One day she looked everywhere and finally found him standing in the bathtub behind the shower curtain. When she came in the room he stuck his head out of the shower curtain and said, "Woof." Toby is smart, and his children are like him. It is Layla, his daughter, who was selected National Therapy Dog of the Year.

And true to form, Layla is not well behaved at home. She also demonstrates the same planning ability, waiting for the right window of opportunity. At an obedience-training session Layla was to sit in a lineup of other dogs while the owners walked out of sight. Before she'd begun the training session, Layla had been eye-ing a barn on the property. In her sit position she continued to eye the barn. When the owners returned, stood still, and called in one voice, "Come," all the other dogs raced to their masters' feet. Layla made a beeline for the barn. She'd been planning ahead, waiting for the right moment. She was trying to accommodate both obedience and dog curiosity at the same time. I think, at least for Toby dogs, thinking for themselves reduces their good-ness factor. A Newf like Ben thinks for me, not for himself. I have great respect for independent dogs like Toby and Layla. They are exciting creatures, but far more difficult to live with.

Toby grew to be impressive enough to win points, attract breed bitches and puppy buyers. (We soon found he did not pass on the funny front to his new puppies.) Every puppy buyer who has come to see our dogs wants one like Toby. Women simply stand with him for twenty minutes, half an hour, stroking, stroking, stroking, Toby leaning up against them, pushing ever so slightly, rolling his eyes up and staring at them. For the dozens of women who have admired him, taken him for walks, stroked him endlessly, Toby has sex appeal. He is a hunk. As Newfies will, he looks in people's eyes as long as they look into his. Other dogs will look for a moment, then glance away. It is as if he's drinking from your soul. It is utterly romantic. In fact, if any-thing is truly outstanding about Toby, it is his lovely disposition, which, it would turn out, he would throw to his progeny.

∞

Newf owners drop in to see the puppies and we sit talking in the dining room. Because the whelping box is in the den, the den furniture has been moved into the dining room, which is crowded now with extra chairs and a sofa. Ben and Toby are with us, lying on the floor at our feet. There is some offense, some slight. Perhaps in my ignorance, Molly's hormonal smell, her leaks and drips and emptying out, those smells on me, whatever, have turned them on. Perhaps the strange configuration of the furniture in a different room worries them. Perhaps, and I consider this the most terrible and likely, Toby knows, just as he knew I had been zapped by radiation, that Ben has cancer. Toby once again finds the window of opportunity. Without a growl of warning, he jumps Ben with a fierce roar, overpowers him, throws him on his back, rips up his ear, his neck. I have never seen such violence. It is a horrible thing to see your pets, your soul mates, as beasts. They are. They have drives and instincts that don't fit into our lives. We shake and weep and scream and pull tails and testicles, choke collars. Nothing stops them. I throw water. My screams, our shouts, only inflame the dogs. The four of us, two men and two big women, cannot separate them. Finally they separate on their own accord.

Three years, almost daily, Toby accepted Ben's discipline, stood still with head dropped while Ben mounted him from the rear and held him in place. There was not a growl or a bite from either dog. "Don't knock Molly over again. Be gentle with that puppy. Don't get so wild. That food belongs to Pippa." When Ben felt he had told Toby how to behave, he would give one warning growl and slide off. Toby would shake himself and walk away, and it was over. He was Ben's charge and duty. Toby had shown respect to Ben from the day he first came to our home. At eighteen months Toby already towered over Ben by four or five inches and twenty pounds. Eventually Ben couldn't reach a mounting position from the rear and had to mount Toby from the front so that Toby's great jaws hung just at Ben's private parts. Even so, good Toby stood still, gently accepting the discipline.

I tried to anticipate every move, every emotion, and fairly well avoided conflict between them. When the ladies came into heat and the testosterone ran high, we were careful to separate the boys and send the females off to a boarding kennel. When I distributed bones from the butcher, I put the boys in separate kennels. We had owned two Labrador retrievers, brothers, who never fought. I had hoped to create the same atmosphere with the Newfs as I had had with the Labs. There are Newf breeders who are able to keep their males together. I understand that if I had brought Toby in as a young puppy and presented him to Ben as his charge and never interfered in Ben's disciplining of Toby, the relationship might have worked. But Toby entered too late, and I knew too little. One nationally known trainer for whom I have the greatest respect told me, "Don't interfere, let them work it out; don't interfere." Another said, "Interfere." Another said, "Don't interfere, you'll be hurt." So far Ben's disciplining of Toby had appeared safe.

I suppose it was inevitable that Toby would reach maturity and decide he was ready to run the show rather than be a bachelor. Now, the birth of the puppies having disturbed the household in a thousand ways, all the ladies in heat or coming into heat, Molly reeking of hormones, and Toby having had real stud experiences, he and Ben are on edge. Neither Ben nor I would let him near the bitches, Ben being far more protective/possessive. Perhaps all those gentle times he stood still with Ben mounted on him, Toby was only biding his time, planning that moment, watching, measuring skillfully that small window, solving the problem of Ben's leadership.

Certainly I have never seen such violence from Ben. I suppose Toby thought this was his chance to take over the family and the territory, and he had to take it as best he could. Whatever, Toby, it seemed, was out for the kill. This, the gentlest, most loving of my dogs. But his primitive nature told him he was a bachelor dog and it was time to find a family. Since he couldn't, as bachelor apes do, wander off into the wild to find a willing female, Toby fought Ben for his family. I understand it, but I feel betrayed to the core of my being.

With a shaking hand I drop four drops of Rescue Remedy under their tongues and under my tongue as well. I pat their heads and necks and ears with paper towels to find the wounds. Toby is whole; Ben is not. We speed Ben to the vet's, where he sits still, without anesthetic, while the vet staples his ear together. Toby is no longer Ben's puppy, no longer the child. He has reached his manhood and needs his own home so deeply that something ancient, terrible, necessary has surfaced.

Ben had never drawn blood on Toby. He was disciplining, not fighting for domination. This violence, this urge for reproduction, this original "kill the king," is a necessary part of living with animals. If Toby had won, if he had taken over the family of dogs, if overcoming Ben had been accomplished, it is entirely probable that Toby would have become exactly as noble and generous and responsible as Ben had been. If I had had the courage or the stupidity—there are strong arguments on both sides—to let Toby win, he might have remained in the family.

I weep for us all, for the biological pieces of life that wound us, that drive us, that bring us to do to others what is so cruel, so necessary. If Ben only has a few months of life left to him, months that may mean weakness and pain, I owe him those months in peace. As much as we adore him, as proud as we are of him, as hopeful for his championship and his stud fees, Toby, whose puppies everyone wants, will have to go to a home where he doesn't have to fight for his dominance. It will be a death, a grief, a terrible thing. But blood has been let. I cannot bear the possibility that he would tear Ben to pieces. And I know Ben will never relinquish his responsibility without fighting to the finish. I can't sacrifice aging Ben to Toby's instinctual and necessary young male violence.

I am heartbroken. I weep not so much over the wounds as over my own failure to give enough love so there would be no hurt. I had lost control. I had thought somehow I could handle the boys, that my love, my devotion, their temperament, could bypass the inevitable territorial competition. I failed. I had worked very hard with Toby for three long and often difficult years. I weep for what will be Toby's confusion when I leave him, his fear, his loneliness. It is my own loneliness I weep for. I couldn't reach out far enough for Toby. Perhaps if Ben weren't so close to me, my first Newfy, perhaps then Toby and I could have become truly close. But there is room for only one lead male.

My middle child, who is mad for Toby and who, according to Toby, smells like me, has just lost a great male Newfy, Bruiser, to cancer. I offer her Toby. He'll be lonely without his family. I can't bear the thought of Toby having once again to adjust to another home, to be thrown out because he was acting naturally.

Toby has to go someplace where he can be number one. She will, my daughter promises, be his dog family. I take Toby on the four-hour trip to my daughter's house, stay with him, try not to show my sorrow, drive home with him, drive down again, leave him for a few days. We plan to pick him up at the end of the week. Each time he stays will be longer.

Now that Ben has decided Toby is gone, something strange is happening. Ben is playing, which is good news and bad news. It means that Toby's presence was a burden for Ben, an enormous responsibility to keep Toby in line, to protect his family. And I am ashamed that I deprived Ben in so many ways. But I am thrilled to see him playing. As I watch him, he drops into a play bow before his daughter Ishtar, surprising her. She moves away. Play is a new behavior for Ben. His family doesn't know quite how to react. Ben follows Isthar, performs a play bow again. This time she accepts his invitation by stacking herself up, bowing, breaking into a run. He springs forward and chases her. They race in huge loopy circles around the lawn, so fast, so low, their belly hairs sweep the grass. The other dogs watch and join the race. Ishtar stops, pivots, zigs and zags, stops. They leap together in great loving tangos, hold, drop, run again. Ben keeps up with her. He has dropped his solemnity. All this time he'd been watching Toby, wary, protective. As I watch Ben play, I know it's the correct decision to let Toby go. It probably was a very incorrect decision to bring him into the household. All the dogs are chasing, racing, pivoting, sprinting in Ben's great circles around the lawn. I don't know how long I can keep Ben alive but today he is very much alive. I feel guilty that he had to be the older dog, the patriarch. He looks young on the lawn, vital, strong, as beautiful as he's always been. The chemo, the herb teas, the homeopathics, the not-quite-legal chemicals, the odd and effective protocol we've worked up from a dozen sources are working for Ben. He's fat and glossy. His eyes are clear and bright. His appetite is good and I have hope. We entered Ben in a match once. A match is like a dog show but there are no points. Ben came in second of all the dogs, of all the breeds. The judge said to me, "I know nothing about Newfs but he's beautiful when he runs."

Flowers bloom, fade, give way to seed. I don't know how I will live without Ben. When Toby returns for a few days on his last visit to my house, Ben retreats, is silent, watchful, lies by the gate, watches. He may be afraid. My daughter comes to get Toby. The danger is over.

Celeste is a mini-Newf. Stunted by steroids, she has only reached the size of an eight-month-old. At three months Rosie and Silky are quickly catching up to her. Celeste is very short. Her front is well developed but crooked, her rear weak and bent. She is as crippled as her sister Ishtar's movement is perfect. She has Ishtar's magnificent head, a solid barrel chest, and angelic clouds of white hair, but her body is dwarfed. Strange long Lhasa apso hair flows down her back. Something went wrong in Celeste's first days. Infant pups who can't use their legs and continue to swim across the whelping box when they should be up on their legs are called "swimmers" and have to be forced up on their legs. So, according to directions from other breeders who had swimmers, we built a swing for Celeste, wrapped a soft cloth around her belly, and suspended her for a few minutes every hour so her legs would just touch the ground. We put her in a tub of warm water to support her body and force her to use her legs. Afterward I would wrap her in warm towels and rub and hold her until she was dry. Exhausted, she would drop off to sleep against me. She hated the water, hated the swing. I can remember her screams, my horror, my confusion, my giving up, trying again. Finally she was able to lift off the ground. Later we would find she was not a "swimmer puppy" at all. Her rear leg muscles weren't developed, either through an embryonic failure or a disease in the muscles. We took every test and could find nothing aclinical in the X-rays or the blood or the enzymes in the muscles. Since she was a breech birth and very difficult to pull, I have always suspected her muscles were simply torn as she was being drawn from the birth canal by her rear legs. No one knew.

We put Celeste through misery. As she reached two months, three months, I watched her front legs overdeveloping, bending under the weight of her body. She used her rear legs but her movement was really dependent on the strength of her front legs. We began a course in acupuncture. I can barely admit now I was party to the medieval torture she was put through. Acupuncture shouldn't, doesn't, hurt; we've done it on the other dogs. This poor puppy screamed her heart out. It was torture. It didn't work.

I begged for help. The vet, troubled as well, would call me at eleven or twelve at night and say, "I was just thinking about Celeste. Maybe we should try . . ." Everything functioned, but her rear legs, although not useless, were not strong, and her development was seriously curtailed. Her back was roaching under from the pain. She was far less active than Ishtar. People offended us deeply by telling us to put her to sleep. I couldn't. Perhaps I will be tougher if the situation, whatever it was, occurs again, but it was my first litter. I had brought her into the world, helped to create her life. I owed her. Heartsick, we waited until she was six months old, then put her on steroids. She lost the swelling and joint pain. Her back straightened out. She could move. But she was already bent and twisted and damaged. "Her future is compromised," the vets declared. The steroids stopped her growth. Her black muzzle turned gray. Her coat continued to grow in long, silken strands. She became a long-haired bearded mini-Newf, uncomplaining, courageous, loving, and, amazingly, after all we'd done to her, completely trusting.

When I was studying gorillas at the Calgary Zoo, I watched a young female named Dongay who was also stunted, who was also quick and socially skilled within her family. Dongay was curious, into everything, completely a part of the gorilla family which was very similar to our dog family. I was fascinated to see that the social development was similar for both Celeste and Dongay. Although they were the smallest in the families, neither of them was treated as a runt, an inadmissible, or a victim. Like Celeste, little Dongay was barrel-chested, nimble and clever. Like Celeste, Dongay was not as strong as the large females, and like Celeste, she had developed very efficient competitive strategies.

∽∞∾

It is a wet early spring day. The paths once trampled in the snow are now muddy trenches, the terraces slides, and the spring water streaming from the base of the willow tree down to the lake is muddy and delicious. Rosie and Silky are as vital and promising as spring itself. At four months, growing steadily, Silky looks like a tenor from a barbershop quartet, his black head parted up the center by his white blaze. Not quite house-trained, but certainly paper-trained, faced with the dilemma of being in the house and having to urinate, he lifted a computer sheet from the wastebasket, laid it down before the fireplace, and peed on it. He thinks the way Ben thinks: applying what he knows to what he doesn't know, stretching to do things right. I have high hopes for him but his physical development is very slow. It will be years before he can go in the ring.

Rosie is gorgeous and well developed. In two months she'll go into the ring. They weigh nearly fifty pounds now, perhaps more at this moment because they are coated in mud from the stream under the willow. Exulting as they are in the mud's texture, coolness, the glory of its splash, they race up and down the stream. There is no white fur showing on them. I call everyone up to the porch for a noontime delicacy of roasted turkey feet. I'm surrounded by mouths. I give the turkey feet to Rosie and Silky first, because if in their puppy frenzy they were to grab a morsel from the vicinity of a grown dog's mouth, they might be disciplined very harshly. Mouths full, the puppies run off to chew in a safe solitary corner and the other dogs receive their horrid treat. I feed Celeste last because she eats faster. Celeste eats faster and thinks faster than the other dogs. Of them all, she is the craftiest. Molly stands over Silky, bullies him with the shadow of her presence. She wants his turkey foot as well as her own and stands over him, breathing heavily. Silky defends his treasure, barks at her. But when his back is turned to face Molly's intrusion, Celeste grabs Silky's turkey foot. Crooked legs and barrel body notwithstanding, Celeste races across the lawn toward the safety of the kennels and the shadows of a doghouse. Molly, who considers herself first in line and deserving of everything, allows Celeste to get away with the turkey foot. Molly has had three litters since Celeste was born. Nevertheless Celeste is still the baby, still the only one Molly grooms, the only one whose ears she cleans, the only one who can take advantage of Molly. Celeste is four. She is a grown dog but we all continue to baby and spoil her.

Poor little Silky wanders around rather aimlessly, looking for his turkey foot in the mud. I watch Silky approach Ben, lick Ben's lips, ask for Ben's turkey foot. Ben ignores him. Silky lies down in some mutually determined acceptable distance from Ben and watches for fallout. Weeks ago, when Silky first presented himself to Ben, Ben growled and would not receive him. Silky persisted, establishing finally a safe distance Ben would tolerate. As the weeks went by, Ben allowed Silky to come closer and closer and finally allowed Silky to lick his lips, to pay respect. Silky adores Ben. That is perhaps too human a term to use. If a boy acted toward a man as Silky acts toward Ben, I could say the boy adored the man. Silky watches everything Ben does, follows him, pulls on Ben's ears, lies beside him, greets him with a frenzy of joy that must be love. If all the dogs are in a space, Silky immediately seeks out Ben, not his mother, or his sister, or me. If Ben is stretched out, Silky stretches out. If Ben is curled up, Silky curls up. If Ben gets up to leave, Silky gets up.

Ben, now that Silky has moved into his presence, seems to

have accepted the responsibility of this puppy who insists on being a friend. He watches Silky, moves close to him if he's too wild or jumping a female or a play moment turns too rough. Ben will stand still, wait for Silky to sense his presence. Silky then ends his disapproved activity, apologizes by licking Ben's lips, and, with clear restraint, walks away slowly from the scene of his crime, carefully looking over his shoulder to see if Ben is following. And Ben is. Rosie shows no interest in Ben in the house, but outside she races to greet him, kissing him with the same frenzy Silky employs. Rosie has attached herself, however, to Pippa. She does what Pippa does. Silky does what Ben does. Molly, their mother, is not a player except for rare moments when she'll chase them, roll them over, and fight with them, as if teaching them. But the new relationships in the kennel are Silky and Ben, Rosie and Pippa.

Ben finishes his turkey foot. Silky examines the ground around Ben meticulously. I take Silky inside and give him peanut butter on oat bread. Celeste returns from her kennel house and examines each circle of grass where the other dogs ate their turkey feet.

The steroids have given her arthritis. Often she cries as she comes up the stairs to my bedroom. Sometimes she doesn't come up the stairs. And sometimes she is so angry at her pain, she growls as she runs down the stairs, growls, I know, at her pain. It took me a while to understand that she wasn't growling at the others catapulting down the stairs ahead, behind, and beside her. One morning she was running down the stairs by herself. I heard the growling and realized she was growling at her pain. Not whining at her pain but growling at it, growling it away, threatening it. I've since heard of another female who has a skin problem and barks at her itches. I placed a very low antique carriage bench at the bottom of my bed so Celeste could climb up easily. It is scarred now by her claws. We bought a set of metal folding stairs for the car so she can climb in without too much stretching. On the nights she sleeps in the garage because she finds it too painful to climb the stairs to my bedroom, I warm blankets in the dryer and tuck her in. Often she gets my Eddie Bauer storm coat. She seems to prefer it to blankets and it has my smell. It also, to say the least, has hers. Some days she suffers. On good days she comes down the lawn to the lake with me, tail wagging, greeting everyone with joy and much licking, nipping at my clothes, sticking her head between my knees. On bad days she watches from the terraces, takes a shortcut to the kennels where she knows eventually I shall return, and meets us at the end of our walk. And on worse days she sits on the porch and doesn't meet us on our walk, and I know it's a very bad day, so I take her inside out of the cold or the rain.

When we walk down the lawn she nips at my feet, trying to hold me, to stop me, to get my attention. Reprimanded, sometimes kneed gently in the chest, often spoken sharply to, Celeste substitutes for the nipping by shoving her powerful bony head between my legs as I walk. I understand her needs but her head hurts my legs, so I give her a stick or a ball to keep her mouth occupied. No ordinary stick or ball will do; it must be one I have and have given to her.

⁂

Celeste loves a good play fight. If there is a wrestling match on the ground between two dogs who outweigh her, she'll get right into it. Her jaws are strong enough to break up a tug-of-war over a rope. She leaps between two large dogs, grabs the rope in its middle, and pulls with great strength in a third direction. If she can't get into the hassle, she'll stand within inches and bark high, sharp barks, exacerbating the excitement. I've seen her challenge young, naive Toby, challenge him to chase her by dropping into a play bow, by running at him and then away, growling at him, biting his lips, barking a high-pitched invitation. Finally, when he agrees to play chase and she has him going around in circles, she just stands still while he runs his heart out and then cuts him off with a simple diagonal across his circle. She has learned to snap, to catch things in the air. If someone drops a piece of cookie, she scrambles and gets there before the other dog even knows he's lost it. To describe her as a cripple is unfair. When I whisper the word "rabbit" and everyone takes off down the hill to the woods, Celeste runs right after them, catches up eventually. If Molly barks an alarm and points toward a direction, Celeste is off the porch and running. Her hind legs curve inward, weak and painful, but off she goes, tail wagging, head high, barking with the grand madness and reckless pleasure of the chase and the pack.

Celeste has taught me that a leash works both ways. I had used a leash as a way to keep a dog with me, in check, controlled. If the dog holds the leash in its mouth, I had learned, it was a sign of dominance and should not be allowed. Celeste is rarely leashed because she doesn't stray. She has been trained and obeys. But one day I saw her pick up a bright pink leash and walk around the driveway with it in her mouth, head held high, making believe she was on lead. And then I understood why she grabs me, grabs the hem of my jacket, the cuff of my sleeve, the string on my boot. She creates a tether between us, holding me so I don't stray from her. Now I put her on lead for no practical reason at all. She holds the leash in her mouth, so we are holding each other. She then holds her head high proudly and walks in front of me but doesn't pull me. The leash is both faith and connection.

She knows no life other than that of pain, but she also knows pleasure. I have wondered if she feels sorry for herself or left out. I don't think so. I think she simply accepts and takes what pleasure she can. Her philosophy isn't a bad one.

⸎

A few days after Silky lost his turkey foot to Celeste, it became clear that he had learned an important lesson. A harvester cuts weeds on our lake and often kills fish, churning them up from the bottom. They float into our cove. One particularly fish-rich morning, Silky is the first out onto the dock to check the fish harvest. I watch as he lifts a six-to-eight-inch catfish, takes the head and half the body into his mouth, and, sitting up, starts chewing. It isn't easy to hold the entire fish and open his jaws to chew at the same time. Half the fish hangs from his mouth. Silky, having already lost a turkey foot, thinks through the problem of keeping his catfish. Celeste is barreling down the lawn, headed in his direction, in the direction of his fish. Celeste arrives at the lake, gallops out to the end of the dock, stops dead at Silky's side, sniffs the fish. Without missing a beat, little Silky, whose trunk is not much larger than his fish, sucks up the entire fish and it's gone in a flash. God knows where it went, but it didn't come out and it was gone and Celeste didn't get it. Celeste, undaunted, finds the skeleton of another fish left by seagulls. Deliriously she rolls in it before I can stop her, moistening behind her ears and under her neck with the perfume of rotten fish, in the same places, I realize, women apply their own perfumes. I roll my pant legs to my knees, and take Celeste into the shallow cove to clean her. Her Lhasa apso hair floats out. She looks like a small furry hippo. I splash water on her neck, try to rub out the smells. Does she roll in fish scent to trap and entice? To disguise herself, therefore protect herself as a fish? To attract other dogs in the way women attract men with perfume?

That night, rain drips from the roof onto the balcony; the windows and door are open. It is a cool and luscious night. Ben is stretched out on the tiles of the fireplace. His head and shoulders are on the carpet. It's his belly he must keep cool. Molly lies in front of the doors to the balcony. If it weren't raining, she'd sleep outside on the balcony. Rosie and Silky are too young to sleep in the house. Pippa gets too warm. So they are all in the garage, Pippa playing nursemaid. I hear Celeste climbing the stairs to my bedroom. She climbs slowly and heavily. She stands next to the bed. I reach down and pat her back. She is fluffy and soft. She has had her bath and smells sweet. She pulls at the cuff of my nightgown to greet me, licks my face for permission to climb on the bed. I pat the bed and hear her claws on the carriage bench. She arrives on the bed with my sneaker as a gift, presses it into my face. I thank her and lay it quietly on the floor. Throwing it down would be an insult. I don't know if she knows she looks lovely but I do know the soak in her oatmeal bath soothes her skin and relaxes her. She takes my sleeve again, holds it in her mouth, attaches to me. I tell her she's beautiful and I rub her chest and under her ears. Celeste steps over Ishtar and takes the lower corner of the bed. Ishtar stretches out as if to control more space. Celeste curls between Ishtar's forelegs and rear legs, her head tucked into Ishtar's belly. I touch Celeste, stroke her hair. She stirs, looks up, understands it's just me touching her yet again, always, forever. She rolls over closer to her sister's body and goes back to sleep with her little sigh. My fingers stink of rotten fish. Soon the room stinks. The fishy vapors have overwhelmed her bath perfumes. Pushing her out of the bed after all she'd gone through to get into it would be too cruel. She so needs me. She sleeps comfortably, almost silently. I know how relieved she is to be with me.

⁕

Steroids ultimately kill. They can create arthritis, which they have, weaken muscles, which they have. They also increase appetite. In order to keep Celeste light on her feet, we reduce her diet. She is constantly hungry. Her stomach muscles have already given out from the steroids and she looks fat although she isn't. Steroids also create water retention, adding to her roundnesses. Eventually the medicine will kill her, break her, as the creeping arthritis is now just attesting. Eventually, but not now. Now we're still going up and down those stairs, growling. Now and then she cries out and we hold her and give her an aspirin. Still we see a happy, loving dog. When the bad times are longer than the good times . . . but I cannot bear it. Others will tell me. Others will help. Someday I will have to put her to sleep, let her go, but not yet. Not yet. In the meantime she is brave, even-tempered, adorable, and good. My mother used to joke when she was growing old that she never bought green bananas. We don't know how long Celeste has, but not knowing, we tend to treat her as if every day is important. She and Ben are clearly not going to be our octogenarians.

When my husband faced his cancer operation, he held Celeste in his arms and asked her for her courage. I know she gave it to him. We think of her bravery, her acceptance of us, her trust in us after all the horrors we put her through trying to help her. She still trusts us, she still loves us. She doesn't take walks in the woods with us, but she has her five acres of lawn, her watery cove, the dead fish, her blanket on the porch, her place under the kitchen table, and her Eddie Bauer nest in the garage.

I tell my puppy buyers an old story about a Newfy who chased a train at the same time every morning for years. Every morning the engineer greeted him. The Newf always stopped at his property line. One day the engineer didn't see the Newf, saw him suddenly in front of the train, too late to stop, and killed him. No one could understand why the Newf had changed his habit of running alongside the train after so many years, until the owners confessed that the Newf had, that day, torn a little girl's dress and been beaten for being bad. Who knows what cause and effect operates in a dog's mind? We can only wonder. Had he committed suicide?

I tell this story to all my new puppy owners, not to convince them that the Newf is suicidal, but to convey how deeply sensitive Newfies are, to indicate the high expectations they have of themselves, and to convince the new owners that New-fies struggle all their lives to understand what is good. Watch-ing puppies growing up, watching them becoming civilized and attentive, has nothing to do with teaching them the obedient tricks of sit, stay, and heel. Their crossing the bridge to our lives has to do with caring for us, watching us, learning how they must live with us, what good is. Or are they teaching us what good is? The terrible punishment of a harsh "No!," the soft slap of a rolled newspaper are bleak messages of personal failure. I think, having known my Newfs now as intimately as I have, their goal, their cause for being, their shimmering vision of themselves, is being good to us. If there is anyone in this family of dogs who personifies goodness, it is Ishtar.

❧

Ishtar, our backyard puppy, Ben and Molly's child, our first-born, is now Champion Blue Heaven's Queen of Heaven. She won her final point amid cheers and champagne. As many peo-ple were happy for her as were happy to get her out of the class ring so their own dogs would have a chance. Since fifteen points are the total requirement for a championship and Ishtar's first win a year ago gave her five points at once, she was suddenly and well on her way.

There is a rule of thumb that black dogs beat Landseers in the ring ten to one. Landseer or not, there was no beating Ishtar. Her body, head, bone, and, most particularly, her strong, fluid grace always brought in the points. Until she lost her coat in midsummer, she won show after show. Ringside I would hear people saying, "What an elegant bitch." At one show a high-rolling breeder from Italy offered my handler ten thousand dollars for her. No one knew who I was or cared. I certainly had no kennel, no line, no background. In fact, when two-year-old Ishtar took a ribbon at her first Newfoundland Nationals in Batavia, New York, in 1993, people congratulated the men who'd bred Molly and Ben, Ishtar's parents, as I stood by. I was a nobody, a flash in the pan. Ishtar, however, was astonishing and important. A very old-time handler of Newfies would often pull me over and show Ishtar to someone else, saying, "See this head? This is the traditional Newfy head. Isn't she gorgeous?" I had no name. I was simply on the other end of the leash. My husband and I would look at her in amazement and remind each other she was just our backyard puppy. But it was clear she belonged in a different league, closer to the league of her great-grandfather Pied Piper. That fall she competed in a four-day show and won three of the shows—certainly, I was assured by old hands, a record. She was a major contender. A well-seasoned judge told me, as Ishtar posed with him for pictures: "She's the most beautiful Landseer bitch I've ever seen."

I do not know how to communicate the physical pleasure I take in Ishtar's beauty except that it is the same I take in Ben's. When Ben and Ishtar challenge each other to a play chase with elegant ritual bows, then agree and take off, I am stunned by their grace and power. When they run low in the great loops around the lawn, their bodies taut, stretching out like racehorses, they look alike; their movement has the same power and grace and poise. Watching them, I wonder if what I feel is the same as the rush of lust, of a flesh lust, that men feel for sexy women. My body tingles at the sight of her running around the ring, head high, tail out, moving perfectly.

I love to be at a distance from her so I can see her as others do. If she knows I'm nearby, she races to me, abandoning her dog activities. She must be with me, pressing against me, reassuring herself, rubbing, pawing, licking, possessing me, staring into my eyes without a blink.

❦

When she and her sister Celeste were puppies, Celeste needed so much attention, Ishtar was ignored. I think she worked harder to reach me than I did to reach her. She grew more and more beautiful and athletic as Celeste twisted with her pain and weakness. It seemed unjust to exult in Ishtar. She was undemanding, obedient, unobtrusive, as good as gold. Unlike other pairs of puppies we've brought up, Ishtar was infinitely gentle with Celeste. They carried none of the vicious litter activity with them, did not fight. Celeste was an excellent swimmer. The two of them would swim in the lake in circles, around and around. When Celeste tired (she wasn't using one of her rear legs), Ishtar would let Celeste climb on her back and swim her around.

There are few anecdotes about Ishtar because she has never done anything wrong. Ishtar was almost a year old when I took her to Ben's breeder. He stacked her up—head high, front legs straight, slightly apart, rear legs stretched backward—as one would present her to a judge in a show. Then I trotted with her around the parking lot. "She's perfect," he said. "Really perfect." Her movement was smooth and powerful, as fluid and strong as Ben's. At two, Ishtar's head was already magnificently handsome, her body balanced and muscled. But because of Celeste, there was still no time for Ishtar and certainly no inclination to show her.

One would think by her attachment to me that I had made a great effort to spoil, train, and bond with Ishtar. Not so. She is attached to me as umbilically as Ben is, but Ben was my first Newf, my only Newf, and I had worked hard for the attachment between us. Ishtar, on her own, created the same attachment to me, an attachment so determined and consuming, I would have certainly chosen a lesser degree if I'd had the choice. The great head pushing at my hand to be touched, the huge body sitting on me, the hurt I imagine she feels when I put her into her kennel or end her overactive licking of me with a sharp command or, worse, hide my head under the sheets and become unavailable.

She ultimately became so keyed in to me, so human and undoglike, so attentive to every move I made, she barely knew what to do with, or even cared about, her first litter. Although she licks and cleans me constantly, tirelessly, until I have to stop her, command her to lie down and sleep, she would not lick her puppies, who desperately needed bowels and bladders stimulated. Ishtar offered a few desultory licks toward their faces when we held a puppy before her, but the normally instinctual mother's job was left to us. Ishtar has moved almost entirely beyond her dog nature. Her sister Celeste has been agreeable and loving but hardly obsessed with me. Molly, her mother, has a loving but independent attitude and will, for example, sleep in one place and stay there when I leave the room. Not Ishtar. When I move, Ishtar moves. Ishtar has learned to dance nimbly in front of me, behind me, to keep from underfoot but be with me, determining as soon as she can, sometimes anticipating, my direction. She is courteous, considerate, thoughtful, a Ginger Rogers to my Fred Astaire, firmly attached but never in the way, reflecting my steps. Since Molly is alpha bitch, Ishtar, of course, does not have Molly's power and prerogatives of rank, but she has all the signs of Molly's imperious, judgmental nature, noticeable in her treatment and disdain of Toby and of certain visiting dogs and people. When Molly does someday relinquish control of the family, I suspect Ishtar will take over. It may be that her need to remain with me, close to me, is a hunger not for me, but for the power I represent.

Ishtar's need to be with me can become annoying. If I'm settled in bed and she's asleep next to me and I need a pencil, I choose not to rise because I'll wake her, and I am summarily angry at both of us. When I've left her for a few days, her entire body trembles when she greets me. If I leave the kitchen when she's eating, she'll leave her food and follow me. It is I who am tethered. I return to the kitchen and sit on the sofa. That's what she wants: me in one place. She'll jump on the sofa, lay her feet and head on my lap, pin me down. My husband brings her bowl, lays it on my lap. She eats. When she's finished, in order to show me she wants no more food, she'll give a polite little burp, hop around on the sofa, and face away from me. The charades they've devised to help us understand them are remarkable, convoluted, and careful and, I would think, far more precise and determined than our efforts to help them understand us. I remove the bowl from my lap and she stretches out again. "Well," I say when I've been there too long, "work time." Graciously she hops off and our day begins. My life is Ishtar's career.

Mid-April, Ishtar's championship two weeks old, we drive with Ishtar and Pippa to Michigan to the Newfoundland Club of American National Competition. When Lewis and Clark's expedition headed westward with their Newfoundland, they had nothing on us. I drive westward in a convoy of Newf vans, loaded with Newfies. Our roofs are webbed with black rubber bungee cords holding down extra crates, exercise pens, coolers. Our Rubbermaid storage chests are loaded with shampoos, body dressings, mousses, rinses, eye wipes, towels, hair dryers, food, water from home, clothing for any weather, provisions beyond provisions, and the full knowledge that anything we need we'll be able to buy on the site from vendors traveling the same roads we are. I have sunscreens, icebags, powders, and lotions for every kind of insect, any kind of medical situation. I have everything. Ishtar brings her soft lamb squeeze toy. When we finally pull into a Red Roof Inn outside Cleveland, a dozen or more Newfy vans are lined up outside the rooms. In the dark we find one another walking dogs behind bushes, lifting excrement with plastic bags. We babble about who we have with us, this puppy, that dog. If we don't know one another, we certainly know of one another and most certainly know about one another's dogs. It is the beginning of the excitement and the fun. The dogs are excited as well.

Ishtar and Pippa are sophisticated dogs. They know how to ride elevators, how to behave in motel rooms: "Sit if strangers want to pet. Wait while she puts out the food and the water. One walk on the grass in the dark . . . she keeps rushing us . . .

and to bed." They both lie down between the two beds in the room, heads facing the door, protectively. Now and then a Newfy calls, a low, unmistakable woo-woo-woo, almost wolf-like. "I am here. Where are you?" My dogs call back. The calls lift from the rooms up and down the Red Roof Inn, a communal pleasure we are all taking. Ishtar and Pippa check my breathing at night. Satisfied, they sigh and lie down in their places between the beds.

Early in the morning, most of us wearing our ski jackets over nightgowns, we rub our eyes and dream of coffee as the dogs kick up dew in tall grasses, watch each other, greet each other nose to nose. On a trip with the dogs, an accomplished bowel movement is like money in the bank. I often suspect they linger over their task because they've learned that once they've accomplished it, the walk is over and they must return to their crates. But we are too busy to let them sniff and play. We have miles to cover. Convincing Ishtar and Pippa to eliminate on strange ground near strange dogs isn't easy. At last, relieved, we put the dogs in the vans, pack up, and check out. From our distances we call out to one another, "Safe trip," and the convoy is off. We drive into the blank, overheated midwest sky. The week will either produce terrible heat or ugly rains.

As we approach the show grounds late that afternoon— a resort lodge in the Upper Peninsula of Michigan's lake country—full-size plywood Newfy cutouts point the way. The dogs recognize the two-dimensional plywood as a Newf, bark and bark at each signpost until we pull in. We set up safari style near woods, under a spreading tree, tents, exercise pens with tops, sunscreens, pails, rugs, our chairs, our vans forming a break. It's animal world; it's Africa. I don't want to go near the civilized spots of hotel or the adjoining motel units, the golf course, the airstrip. I want to stay outside, in the wild, with the Newfies. The Newfies are now three-dimensional, everywhere—on leads, in braces, in exercise pens, on the front seats of air-conditioned motor homes, in crates under trees. Seven hundred Newfies are here. Other people have tents, campers, cookstoves, state-of-the-art items I immediately want to buy, have, use. We are prepared to camp out. Although we'll sleep in hotel rooms, we'll spend our days outside with the dogs. Most owners leave their dogs in exercise pens or crates in their vans. Ishtar and Pippa will sleep with me in my room.

I want to eat cheese and drink wine and talk to everyone. I am a fool and my dogs are fools, and we are elated to be at the Nationals. People come under our tree to visit, examine our dogs, talk about puppies. We pull our dogs from their pens to show them off. Our visitors "go over" them. It's a flesh market, a primitive tribal affair of examining herds. Breeders feel head, bones, backs, the ratio of pelvis to scapula, the space between forelegs, the height of the hocks on the back legs. "Nice," they say. No one says anything more than "Nice." It is all one can expect. Are they jealous? Honest? What do they really think?

We consider stud dogs and breeding females, trading puppies, leasing bitches to breed. "I need more head. He has a good headpiece." "My bitch has beautiful movement but I need more length in the leg." We are making proposals, possible deals. We'll pay return visits to their camping sites, "go over" their dogs. We are all full of ourselves and our dog news. We are talking dog. It is the ultimate family picnic, a circus. It reminds me of the Fourth of July on Rockaway Beach when I was thirteen, among thousands of people, all with their beach equipment, all splashing in the water, I, young, blooming with my own potential. Now I am blooming with my dogs' potential, my dogs' beauty. I am at a celebration, at a festival. I am as happy as that girl on the beach, perhaps happier since I've now known loss and sadness. Yes, happier. I feel the excitement bubbling in my chest. I want to hug and touch and know everything about everyone's Newfies. It is the ultimate community, the coming together of the tribes. I am nearly drunk on the joy of finding people who love Newfies, of finding Newfies who love people. I am a fool. It's the sixties. It's Woodstock. It's a love fest. My mouth cannot stop. I am not cool at all. I am too noisy, too communicative, too curious, too open. I cannot stop touching other people's dogs. Nor can my dogs. Ishtar and Pippa, feeling the same joyous curiosity as I feel, want to smell behinds, fronts, feet, noses, know everything about everyone, dog and people alike. I hear other owners command: "No sniff." It isn't a command my dogs know. We go into a constant tug mode.

I put Ishtar and Pippa in their exercise pens, clip the sides of the pens together (I think), and leave to register at the hotel. Two hours later, having felt, talked, visited, I return. Ishtar is asleep outside her pen. Had she followed me? I have no idea. I am embarrassed by my ineptness, astonished by her goodness, and very relieved. I suspect she tried to follow me, find me, care for me in the melee of dangers and strangers, could not find me, and returned to the place she knew she should be. I don't know what is in Ishtar's mind but she was happy to see me, content to go back inside the pen. "Watch yourself, Ishtar," I tell her. "There may be some people around here who think you're still a dog."

Ishtar refuses her dinner, refuses her cookie. She avoids eating while she's on the road and loses much too much weight from the stress of change. Primitively and functionally, gorillas defecate before attacking. Ishtar is acting primitively. What are these words: anger, danger, stranger, changes? I'm frustrated. She must eat for strength. I've been at shows with other people's dogs who don't eat for a week. But mine? I offer her everything and anything. She eats nothing. That night, all the Newfies at the encampment start calling to each other. Their voices mingle, spread, retreat, like ocean waves. The women in my condo giggle. It is all I can do to keep myself from calling out, from howling with the dogs.

Ishtar is honored. Chosen because of her body, she is asked to appear before judges who are learning the Newf standard in order to qualify as judges of Newfs. A black male appears with her as an example of a fine Newf. I know there and then I will breed with him. Two major kennel owners go over Ishtar, talking about her fine points, her bone, her head, her balance. I am inordinately proud of her. When I'm asked who her parents are, I say it was just a backyard breeding. After all, Molly and Ben are unknowns, without championships. Graciously one of the kennel owners responds that it depends on what you have in your backyard.

⟨∞⟩

What is a dog show? It's part beauty contest, part athletic event, part flesh market. It is really all about breeding: finding the right male and the best female. A show is hundreds of vans, trucks and tents. It is thousands of nervous dogs, handlers, owners, grooming tables, hair dryers, sprays, shampoos, crates. The grooming areas, always jammed, surround the rings. Vendors set up booths nearby to display dog food, toys, grooming aids, photos, antiques, mats, crates. It is all this and the competition to show off your dog, to take home a ribbon, and, for the very few among us, to win.

The competition will take four days. First there will be the class dogs (those not yet champions). Puppy dogs compete on day one; puppy bitches on day two. Then the more serious competitions begin. Grown dogs compete and then grown females compete. Winners of these competitions, even though they are not yet champions, will enter the ring on the final day with the champions. It is this event, the Intersex, the competition of champions, both male and female, for which everyone waits. The winner of the Intersex is the Best of Show. There will be a Best of Opposite Sex winner—female if a male wins, male if a female wins—and up to five Award of Merit dogs and five Award of Merit bitches chosen. I am thrilled that Ishtar will go into this noble ring. I have no expectation other than the pleasure of watching her in the company of great dogs.

The day of the Intersex is already too warm. I've given Ishtar over to the woman who will show her: Terry White from Kiowa, Colorado. Showing a dog is a fine-tuned performance for dog and handler, together. The handler understands the dog's best points, can display these, can cover her faults, and, in Ishtar's case, can move her at such a pace that her movement—Ishtar's outstanding feature—will be best presented. Terry is shy, cool, confident, or at least looks that way. She bathes Ishtar in an outdoor area, dries her, trims her feet, ears, brushes her out. I stay away. And I'll stay out of sight at ringside. This is the biggest moment in the Newf world. Photographers are everywhere. There's Bruce Weber on a platform, waving, pointing, telling me to meet an editor from *The New Yorker* magazine. He's already photographed Ishtar and Pippa for hours. K9TV has set up under a beach umbrella. Everyone has videos and cameras. I don't. I expect nothing. It is enough to have my baby in this show, rubbing shoulders with major dogs and bitches, in the big time. This is the big time. And then it's show time. Trying to catch a view of Ishtar I wander back and forth. I see Terry's green skirt in the crowd of dogs and handlers. It's a bright, sunny eighty-five- to ninety-degree day, not a good place for dogs in fur coats. Ishtar has an advantage over the black dogs: she won't absorb the heat quite as much as they.

Ninety champions will enter the ring. Everyone unfolds beach chairs and umbrellas at ringside positions for the best view. The dogs and their handlers assemble under the tent. The judge has intentionally set the show site uphill since these are working dogs and must demonstrate drive and stamina. The judge is an all-breed judge, enormously respected, having been in the ring and admired for many years. She's seen everything. She has a benign face under an angelic pouf of white hair. She herself stands straight and proud, is gracious and courteous to everyone. It's her ring and she's in full control. We wonder how she can possibly judge ninety dogs and remember which ones she likes. She holds no pen or paper. Winnowing out the winners will be a monumental task.

The show schedule is always tight. The floor is always too crowded. Owners and handlers stand around the ring, nervously brushing their dogs' imaginary tangles, keeping the dogs from sitting on their perfectly groomed tails, keeping their tails out of the sawdust, keeping them away from other sniffing, drooling dogs. A dog gets no more than a few minutes in the ring, ready or not. Confidence, structure, and movement are the criteria the judge measures. There is no room for poor performance or errors. The dogs are positioned for the judge's examination: head high, neck long, rear legs stretched out, front legs straight. After they've been examined, the judge asks the handlers to trot the dogs around the ring. Then, one by one, each dog is more carefully examined: teeth, testicles, tail set, ear set, topline, length of tail, length of ear, width of bone. The judge will often demonstrate the dog's faults to the audience by pausing for a moment over a poor topline or running her hand along a tail that is too long, a nose too sniped, ears too short. She is judging Ishtar against a standard, a perfection of detail. Ishtar's fault is her ticking, the black dots showing up along her flank. It is her only fault. I am quite sure she will be dismissed early on in the competition. But faults can be forgiven. It is the affect in the ring, the show, the movement, the presence of a dog that lifts it into the winner's circle. Movement and beauty are the coins of this realm.

The champions are brought out from under the tent and the entire incredible group runs along the judge's field. They are breathtaking, all of them, powerful, gorgeous, and there's my girl. I duck behind an umbrella as Ishtar enters the ring. She's looking for me, scanning the crowd. Terry chucks her under the chin and they start out, building into a solid, even trot. I watch her trot through a gamut of threatening dogs, strange legs, ladies, men, sawdust, flapping banners. There are no dogs or people in the ring Ishtar knows. She must feel the anxiety: a cluster of people who distrust one another, aggressively competitive, ambitious, with ninety strange dogs feeling the tension at the other end of their leads. I remind myself that these are the finest dogs in the country, in many countries. I'm conscious only of Ishtar. There is a breeder's fever called kennel blindness: only your dogs look good. I am completely biased. I am here only to see Ishtar. The moment has cost me thousands of dollars, years of care, diet, training, exercise, love. I watch the others politely. Onlookers are marking their catalogs, making notes on bone and build, movement, heads. I'm not. I am here for Ishtar's moment.

Ishtar has known Terry White, her handler, for two days. All response, Ishtar throws her head up, stays right with Terry, does whatever Terry's movements and collar jerks ask of her. She stretches out and moves hard and powerfully. She does not lag, slump, look behind her, falter, drop her head. She holds that proud head up, that tail straight, those eyes slightly crossed, as if looking inward for strength and courage. She moves. I love the moment. I can finally see her. Oh, she moves beautifully.

The woman from *The New Yorker* is asking me questions. I have to excuse myself, to be alone, to feel the fullness of this moment. Ishtar looks good. She is performing. She is very good, very impressive. My friends give me a thumbs-up. She is concentrating, her long tongue tucked in, only a little heart-shaped pink curve showing, her tail out straight, head up high, neck long and strong, proud, alert, concentrating. My beautiful baby, my gorgeous elegant bitch I pulled from between her young mother's legs, who grew up in my laundry room, who sleeps on my bed and eats on my lap, with whom I am intimate, Ishtar, out there, my winner. She knows what she's doing; she knows what's expected of her. She is good.

The dogs return to the tent. Now, one by one they are brought out for the judge's inspection. The judge goes over each dog, head, legs, tail set, length of ear, topline. She is very fast, very accurate, very precise. She indicates with a wave of her hand that the handler trot the dog on the course. We watch as the dog approaches, watch the straightness of his front, the power of his body, the width of shoulder. Some dogs of little substance are disguised under heavily groomed and sculptured coats. The proper brushing and cutting can produce better angulation in the rear, a wider chest, a smooth topline. None of the poufing fools the judges but the overall look, false or not, is impressive. Some of the dogs are not sculptured with scissors and mousse. What you see is what you get.

A dog known to be aggressive, who lunged once at a judge, has just bitten a steward and should be completely disqualified, crosses the field, so sloppily, his tongue dangling long and loose from the side of his mouth, that we are certain he's been drugged. He looks terrible. Another dog who we know has a poor body, throws bad puppies, and simply doesn't have structure nevertheless looks gorgeous going around the ring. He's a real performer and performance counts. There's the bad elbow problem on that one. There's the weak rear. There's the powerful front, the wonderful coat, the massive head. It takes us a few beats to understand that the judge crosses her arms over her chest as a signal to a note taker sitting behind her in the shade of the tent.

And then it's Ishtar's turn to be presented to the judge.

Ishtar doesn't have enough hair to be sculpted, but she has nothing to hide—no soft topline, no crooked legs, plenty of powerful bone. Her structure is still perfectly balanced. She is straight and true. Terry stacks her up before the judge. Ishtar stands under the blazing sun, examines the judge's face and eyes as the judge examines her bone for bone, muscle for muscle. I know every bone and muscle, every curl of hair, ears, nipples, tail, toes. I have felt, touched, stroked every bit of her. She has unfortunately lost so much of the soft flowing white hair that normally covers her ticking, she looks very spotted. The judge smiles down at her, signals for her to run the course, and crosses her arms. Ishtar runs away from the judge, up the incline, across the field, down toward the judge. The judge watches her until she is back in the shade of the tent, crosses her arms, then bends to the next champion.

She's made the cut. Ishtar, my puppy girl, is still in the competition. She and the remaining dogs and bitches (about half of the original field) again stand in the sun, run uphill, across the top of the hill, down toward the judge, and the judge once again goes over them. Again Terry presents Ishtar to the judge. The judge again smiles at Ishtar, crosses her arms. I cannot sit still. Just being in the ring is honor enough; having made the first cut is honor enough. And now Ishtar has made the second cut. The field narrows. The dogs and bitches who have not made this next cut race around the ring to the crowds' applause. Ishtar and Terry wait in the shade with the dogs and bitches who have made the cut. "She looks great," a friend whispers. Another says, "I've bred for twenty-five years and never gone this far." Only from their remarks do I really begin to understand what Ishtar has accomplished. I wander to different points at ringside, hide behind people, talk to no one. I want to savor every iota of this moment.

After each cut Ishtar is still in the competition. I can see how tired she is by the increasing length of her tongue. I know how good she is being. Judges are generally biased about color: they prefer blacks. Ishtar is the only Landseer making the final cuts, male or female. The judge crosses her arms for Ishtar again and again and again. I don't remember how many cuts there are. I am euphoric. My backyard baby, my first breeding, stayed in there with the big-timers, the kings and queens from the major kennels that breed dozens of dogs a year. These kennels own and co-own dozens of champions to send into the ring at the Nationals. She is beating generations of skilled and managed breedings, major kennels. She is my little miracle; I can take no pride, only joy. I bite back tears. How I wish for a phone nearby so I can call my husband.

The crowds increase. The judge is ready to make her final selections. She chooses the Best of the Breed. Owners and handlers scream, hug, weep. Then the Best of Opposite Sex. She walks up and down the line of dogs and bitches. She signals to Terry to go up to the top of the line with the winners. Bruce yells to me from his platform: "I've got plenty of footage, don't worry." Ishtar has been selected by the judge for an Award of Merit. I weep into my hands. People are hugging me. I'm surrounded by well-wishers. The judge selects only two other females. She could have selected five others but doesn't. And there's my girl running around the ring with the most beautiful Newfs in the world and she's one of them. The crowd is cheering and I'm crying and I don't really get it, any of it, or how it could be, but it is. Terry grins as they run up that hill again, for the last time. And the Newfy Nationals are over.

⁓

"Good girl," I say again and again to Ishtar when I have her alone in the motel room, after she'd drunk cups of water. "Good, good girl." She knows she has my approval. Winning means nothing. Ishtar was being good in the ring. She licks my lips, my cheeks, my hands, nuzzles, presses hard into me. I offer her a biscuit on the gold-and-cobalt-blue Lenox plate she's won. I show her the gold Newfoundland head on the plate and tell her how good she was again and again. She hears the praise in my voice, knows what I am saying to her. But she won't eat the biscuit, even from a gold plate. Always a lady, she backs away from her food, politely, sits at a distance from it, telling me, quite clearly, that she is not about to eat.

Later, a friend talks about Ishtar to the judge, who tells him that she chose Ishtar because she is a sound and true dog, an honest dog with soul in her eyes. She is. She is, after all, Ben's daughter. And then Margaret Willmott, the Topmast breeder, the source of the finest Landseers, tells me that of all the dogs in the ring, Ishtar had the most beautiful movement. She does; she is Ben's daughter. I watch the K9TV film of Ishtar in slow motion moving around the ring. She is magnificent.

Ishtar's American Kennel Club registered name is Champion Blue Heaven's Queen of Heaven. If it is true that the only power of prediction left to human beings is in the naming of their children, we have chosen the correct name for Ishtar.

I put Ben to sleep this morning. Suddenly, swiftly, the cancer attacked him and this time it won. His glands swelled behind his eyes and in his nasal passages. I offered him chicken. Only until I placed it on his tongue did he eat it, ravenously. In the morning I climbed backward down the stairs from my bedroom to the front hall, holding his head, steadying him, leading him down each step, because he couldn't see his way down. His eyes were drooping, ointment for the pain clouding them.

He had stayed with me all night but all night he had panted and drunk gallons of water. He couldn't breathe through his nose and couldn't sleep. Agitated, sleepless, I would hear him crash down, snore a few seconds, and then stand and pant. I put my pillow next to him and lay with him, rubbed his chest. He pressed his head hard on my shoulder, against my neck, taking comfort, lifted his leg so I could reach his favorite spot on his chest. When I poked around in the dark fur to take his temperature, he politely lifted his tail as he had when he was a puppy, so I could see better and hit the correct spot. At last, in the morning he slept briefly on the kitchen floor before I took him to the vet's. I knew he had to sleep. I had promised him when the cancer was first diagnosed I would not let him suffer. Last night he suffered. I knew how tired he was. Two days before he'd been fine, mounting his daughter, eating everything in sight, dashing and splashing into the cove where the ice had melted. He had had perhaps, altogether, in the fifteen months we'd been treating him, three or four bad days. I would not let him have any more. I would not let him be blind or ignoble. I would not let him hurt. I lay on the terrazzo floor with him, holding him. He kept his head between his paws, tried to sleep, rolled his eyes up at me when I spoke, touched me with a paw. I touched every part of him. I know every roll of flesh, valley, crevice, the feel of bone, muscle, each hair on him, have imprinted him so I will always feel him next to me. I would know him blind, every inch of him, and he I. So I covered him with my touches, remembered him, felt him, held him.

"Come back," I told him, and sang his Ben friend song to him. "Ben friend, I love you, my Ben friend." I could barely sing through my tears. He looked at me. He loved his song. "Come back. I'll recognize you by that white foot. Come back, darling, but sleep now. You need to sleep so badly."

And he was asleep, not struggling for air, his face a soft little velvet puppy face with his long velvet ears and rubber nose, his beautiful face, his beautiful soul. "Sleep, darling." I covered him with my body. "Your work is done. Go. When you come back, we'll find those wild strawberries by the railroad bed and we'll walk and walk forever. All the places we've been, Ben, we will still be. Come back soon, Ben. Sleep." It is as if someone had ripped the skin from my body. I have come apart.

The vet was upset, held me when it was over. The nurses sniffled. Newfs are remarkable dogs. Someone asked me once if I'd ever lost a dog. I had, many. "But have you ever lost a Newf?" that someone pressed on. "It's different."

It is. Newfs are remarkable dogs and, of them, Ben was a remarkable Newf, noble and beautiful, as good as gold. Another Newf owner called today in tears. She had to put her dog to sleep. Because she didn't want to remember him dead, she was not going to be with him when he died at the vet's. I told her that she must go, that her dog's final blessing, his final job, is in that moment of death when his soul is released. For at that moment his soul will illuminate her soul and give her his blessing. Ben, I know, gave me his.

Still, I feel him in the night come to the bedside, press his nose into the small of my back, sniff. Later, I turn over and feel the wet tip of his nose against my own nose, reassuring himself that I'm still there, still breathing. I hear him drinking from the toilet bowl, padding back to the bedroom, flopping here, there, back to the tiles of the fireplace skirt. The short little breaths grow steady and more shallow and then he sleeps. At dawn, when the light comes in through the windows, Ben is on his back, spread out, his white chest gleaming in the new soft light. I rise, step over him. He opens his eye, satisfied, goes back to sleep, then realizes I'm leaving and catapults down the stairs before me. I know what tape was played for him when he first came to me. "When I meet her, I will lie down next to her or on her and taste her as much as I can. I will get used to that smell, that taste, that hairless lumpy texture. From now on I will be attached for life. She will give me what I need and more. I will give her what she needs and more. I will protect her from strangers, sadness, pain, loneliness. She is mine. I am hers."

⚜

Years ago in California, Ben's breeder, Allen Ransome, had a call about a Newf whose family had divorced. The husband, furious, had insisted on having the dog because the wife had the children, but afterward he gave the dog up to Newf Rescue, a group that places Newfs in need of homes. The dog had willed himself to die. He would not move, would not lift his head to eat. He was a huge male and couldn't be lifted. The decision was made to put him to sleep. Allen insisted on trying to save the dog. With the help of friends and a borrowed truck, he took him home and went to bed with him. For an entire weekend he slept with him, stroked him, talked to him. Finally, after hours and hours of silence and no movement, the dog lifted his head, looked around, sniffed, thought about where he was, and stood up. He was willing to live. It took Allen months to bring the dog back to health, back to life. When Allen heard about another family that had lost their Newf, whose little girl was brokenhearted, he arranged to meet them with the dog at a show. Allen stood with the Newf at ringside. Suddenly the dog looked up, spotted the little girl at a great distance, stared, watched, completely focused on her approach. There were a dozen or more Newfs at the ring. But the little girl raced to him, hugged him, buried herself in his chest. He nuzzled her, she took his lead, and off they went. Had they recognized each other?

Breeders say you always look for the great one you lost. You watch every puppy in case he's the one. I will. I lost a great one. But I had him. And I'll recognize him. I cry for Ben, not because I lost him, but because he had to leave and I know how much he wanted to stay with me.

Epilogue

As this book goes to print, Rosie and Silky are almost two years old. Rosie has turned into an astonishingly beautiful bitch. She is actually better than Ishtar. She is shown by the most famous of all Newfoundland handlers and is now a champion. I did indeed watch Champion Blue Heaven Rose Blossom in the ring at the Westminster Kennel Club show in Madison Square Garden. My husband says that if Rosie were a woman, she would break men's hearts. Silky has the promise, the magic, but it will take him years to mature, grow coat, pull together all the powerful loose ends. The pound-and-a-half puppy grew to 130 pounds. Ben was indeed Silky's model: Silky is a kind and decent dog who has taken over the family. He doesn't allow fights. He doesn't allow stealing from food bowls. He has almost, almost taken over Molly's role as leader. Molly is beginning to defer to Silky. After the win at the Nationals, Ishtar bred with Champion Fantasea Pretty Boy Floyd, who had come in first at the international dog show last year, a world champion.

They produced a grand litter of show dogs. Pippa went for a honeymoon to the Saskatchewan prairie and came home to deliver an amazingly large litter of thirteen vital Landseer puppies. She was, not unexpectedly, a perfect mother. Toby has earned his Therapy Dog Certification and works with autistic teenagers at the Anderson School in Staatsburg, New York. Celeste, now five, has somehow gained enough strength in her legs once again to climb the stairs and into my bed at night. And Molly, having bred in the fall with a magnificent black dog from Colorado—Champion Irish of Killigrews—produced two black puppies: Blue Heaven's Daisy Daisy, who has Ben's white front paw and the white angel shape on her chest, and a promising male named Blue Heaven's William the Conqueror. We call him Billy. In each ending there is a beginning.

Special thanks for sharing their Newfoundland stories to Sue Osier-Bickel, Christine Gray, Janice Hight, Allen Coit Ransome, Hannah Hayman, and Margaret Willmott.